D0862654

STUDIES IN MODERN GREEK

The Development of the
Greek Language

GREEK EDUCATIONAL SUPPLIES
ΕΛΛΗΝΙΚΟ   ΒΙΒΛΙΟΠΩΛΕΙΟ
164 Bridge Road, Richmond, 3121
Melbourne - Australia
Telephone: (03) 428 7198

books   records   slides   maps   posters   magazines

Studies in Modern Greek

The Greek Folk Songs, Niki Watts (1988)

C.P. Cavafy, Christopher Robinson (1988)

Nikos Kazantzakis—Novelist, Peter Bien (1989)

Dionysios Solomos, Peter Mackridge (1989)

The Development of the Greek Language, Wendy Moleas (1989)

Erotokritos, David Holton (1990)

Seferis, Roderick Beaton (1990)

STUDIES IN MODERN GREEK

◆◆◆

THE DEVELOPMENT OF THE GREEK LANGUAGE

WENDY MOLEAS

BRISTOL CLASSICAL PRESS U.K.
ARISTIDE D. CARATZAS, PUBLISHER U.S.A.

First published in 1989 by:

U.K.
Bristol Classical Press
226 North Street
Bedminster
Bristol BS3 1JD

U.S.A.
Aristide D. Caratzas
P.O. Box 210
481 Main Street
New Rochelle
NY 10802

ISBN 1-85399-058-2

ISBN 0-89241-485-5 (Hbk)
0-89241-486-3 (Pbk)

Acknowledgement is made to the following for the use of copyright material:
Anvil Press Poetry for the translation of *The Axion Esti* by Keeley and Savidis;
Chatto and Windus for the extract from *Wind of Freedom*;
Lawrence and Wishart for the extract from *The Twelve Lays of the Gipsy*;
Oxford University Press for the Makriyannis translation;
Penguin Books for selected translations from *The Penguin Book of Greek Verse*
and for the translation of Cavafy from *Four Greek Poets*.

British Library Cataloguing in Publication Data

Moleas, Wendy
    The development of the Greek language.-
    (Studies in modern Greek)
    1. Greek language
    I. Title   II. Series
    480

Printed and bound by Short Run Press Ltd., Exeter

SERIES PREFACE

This new series of critical studies will make the findings of the considerable research into Modern Greek literature available in a form and at a level accessible to the student, the teacher and the general reader.

These introductory books should be invaluable to those seeking an understanding of, and a critical guide to, the study of some of the most widely read figures of Modern Greek literature. The series has been specifically designed to cater for the needs of those studying for GCE 'A' level Modern Greek in the UK and undergraduates in the UK, Australia and the USA.

The major concerns of each author are examined critically and objectively, and the background, style and language as well as characterisation, where relevant, of the works are discussed.

Special thanks are due to the Standing Committee of Modern Greek in the Universities (SCOMGIU) in the UK for their support of the series from its inception, and to Bristol Classical Press for making its realisation possible.

Niki Watts
Series Editor

Η νέα αυτή σειρά κριτικών μελετών θα κάνει τα ευρήματα της σημαντικής έρευνας που διεξάγεται στον τομέα της σύγχρονης Ελληνικής λογοτεχνίας διαθέσιμα σε μια μορφή και ένα επίπεδο προσιτό στο φοιτητή, το δάσκαλο και το γενικό αναγνώστη.

Τα εισαγωγικά αυτά βιβλία θα είναι χρήσιμα για όσους επιθυμούν να μελετήσουν μερικά από τα πιο πολυδιαβασμένα συγγράμματα της σύγχρονης Ελληνικής λογοτεχνίας και αναζητούν έναν κριτικό οδηγό. Έχουν δε σχεδιαστεί με σκοπό να ανταποκρίνονται ιδιαίτερα στις απαιτήσεις όσων μελετούν Νεοελληνική φιλολογία για τις εξετάσεις GCE 'A' level στην Αγγλία καθώς και των φοιτητών των Νεοελληνικών σε πανεπιστήμια της Αγγλίας, Αυστραλίας και των Ηνωμένων Πολιτειών Αμερικής.

Οι σημαντικότερες επιδιώξεις του κάθε συγγραφέα εξετάζονται κριτικά και αντικειμενικά και συζητούνται η γλώσσα, οι ιδέες και οι χαρακτήρες των έργων.

Θα ήθελα να ευχαριστήσω ιδιαιτέρως την Επιτροπή για τη Διδασκαλία των Νέων Ελληνικών στα Αγγλικά Πανεπιστήμια (SCOMGIU) για την υποστήριξή της, ηθική και έμπρακτη, καθώς και τον εκδοτικό οίκο Bristol Classical Press που ανέλαβε την έκδοση της σειράς.

Νίκη Watts
Εκδοτική επιμέλεια

AUTHOR'S PREFACE

In 1980 I was lucky enough to be given a sabbatical term by the school where I teach and this enabled me to live in Athens for three months and to study for myself the development of the Greek language. I should like to thank the governors of Manchester High School for Girls who made this possible. I had been enjoying works of medieval and modern Greek literature for many years and I wanted to have a closer look at the changes in the language. I obtained permission to use the library of the Department of Linguistics at Athens University and to attend lectures or classes of my choice. These facilities were offered me by the head of the department, Professor George Babiniotis, and I should like to record here my thanks to him and his staff. I am also grateful to the British School of Archaeology in Athens for the use of the library there and to the American School of Classical Studies, whose Gennadius Library is open to anyone who wishes to read, whether for research or simply for pleasure.

When I came to learn modern Greek many years ago, my training in Classics was invaluable. Having learnt for myself how accessible and rewarding the literature of modern Greece is, I want to encourage other classicists to study the modern language. Modern Greek classes are now widely available and students with a knowledge of ancient Greek make rapid progress.

I hope that the book will also be read by non-classicists. Apart from the purely linguistic information, all other sections of the book are self-explanatory and all the extracts have been translated. I make no claim to be presenting a full literary survey but I hope to give a taste of the quality of Greek writing through different epochs and to provide a starting point for further exploration.

I should like to thank Mr John Betts of the Bristol Classical Press for his encouragement and Mr James Hooker of University College London for helping me with the revision of the first chapter.

WENDY MOLEAS
Manchester

CONTENTS

CHAPTER ONE

PREHISTORIC AND ANCIENT GREEK

Greek is one of the family of Indo-European languages and it has the distinction of having the longest history of all European languages. Modern Greek is a direct descendant of the ancient language and a varied but unbroken literary tradition extends from the poetry of Homer in the eighth century BC to the writings of the present day. The basic form of the language has been preserved. Modern Greek is much closer to ancient Greek than most people realise. The structure of the language has been simplified, there have been adaptations of vocabulary and changes in pronunciation, but once these are understood, the modern language is easily accessible. For the Greeks themselves, whatever their difficulties, there has always been the worship of the Orthodox Church to keep their language alive. The Greek world has by no means had an untroubled history. It has seen many changes, particularly in its occupation by foreign powers from the time of its incorporation into the Roman Empire up to the long period of Ottoman rule which only came to an end in the nineteenth century. The language has survived intact and it has also travelled far. The conquests of Alexander the Great in the fourth century BC carried it as far as India and in the twentieth century AD the language is spoken by Greek communities all over the world, with particularly large groups in the USA and in Australia.

The poems of Homer are the earliest works of Greek literature. They were the result of an oral tradition, being composed in the eighth or seventh centuries BC and committed to writing in the seventh or sixth centuries. These dates are not certain but it is important to note that written literature emerged quite late in the time scale of the development of the Greek language. Our evidence for the form of the language earlier than Homer comes from a comparison with other Indo-European languages and from inscriptions. The earliest Greek writings which we now have are the Linear B tablets from the Mycenaean palaces on Crete and

1

the mainland of Greece. These date back to the fourteenth and thirteenth centuries BC; they were discovered at the beginning of the present century and deciphered in the 1950s.

The discovery was made by Sir Arthur Evans when he excavated the palace at Knossos on Crete and found there many clay documents which had been preserved by fires. On these he was able to distinguish three scripts, one of them a pictographic system and two purely syllabic. The syllabic scripts used a system of ideograms and of signs which would have been suitable for representing the sounds of syllables. The two different syllabic scripts had the same number of signs, but they were not identical and their arrangement was different. To distinguish them, Sir Arthur Evans described them as Linear A and Linear B. Neither he nor his followers considered it likely that either script represented the Greek language, even though collections of Linear B tablets were found in large numbers on the mainland of Greece at Pylos, Mycenae, Tiryns and Thebes. According to the established theory of their time, Sir Arthur Evans and other contemporary scholars maintained that Bronze Age Greece was a province of Crete and any writings found from that period would be non-Greek. It also took a long time for the Linear B scripts to be published and thus the final decipherment was delayed for nearly fifty years. We now know that the Linear B script represents the Greek language. The Pictographic and Linear A scripts are still undeciphered but they probably represent the language of the pre-Greek Minoans.

When the breakthrough was made, it shed a completely new light on the world of the Mycenaeans and, for the first time, it was possible to speak about Mycenaean Greek. The inscriptions consist of lists and records of transactions and there is no evidence of any literary use. Credit for the decipherment goes firstly to an American scholar, Dr Alice Kober, who in the late 1940s distinguished sign groups which showed grammatical inflection and made suggestions about the phonetic relationships of the signs. Her work was followed by that of the Englishman, Michael Ventris, who presented conclusive proofs that the language was Greek. Using a series of grids and statistical analyses, he worked out a system of grammar and word-groupings. One grouping, that of words for towns, was particularly useful for decipherment as it could be tested with known place names. For example, having deciphered Amnisos, Ventris also identified Knossos and Tylissos, using the analogy of the ending –so. Then two common totalling words to–so (masculine) and to–sa (feminine) were identified, corresponding to Greek τόσο / τόσοι and τόσα / τόσαι.

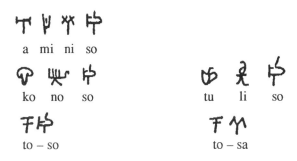

Similar analogies produced many more Greek forms and a joint work by Ventris and John Chadwick, published in 1953, became the basis of all later studies. Tragically, Michael Ventris was killed in a car crash in 1956. The whole story can be read in John Chadwick's book *The Decipherment of Linear B*.[1]

The principal elements of Linear B are syllabic signs, ideograms, signs for weights and measures and numerical signs.†

The script is written from left to right. Each sign represents an open syllable and a consonant which closes a syllable is generally ignored, e.g. a–pi = ἀμφί, ka–ko = χαλκός. Where two consonants are in sequence, the first is expressed with a dead vowel, eg a–mi–ni–so = ᾿Αμνισός, ku–ru–so = χρυσός and po–ro– = προ–. There are several ambiguities. Neither aspiration nor the length of vowels is shown, the same sign represents both 1 and r, and s or n at the end of a word is not shown. The three examples of texts or sections of texts shown below are taken from James Hooker's book *Linear B, An Introduction*.[2]

1. to–sa   pa – ka – na   sword   50   (τόσα φάσγανα)

This tablet is from the Corridor of the Sword Tablets at Knossos. Although 'sword' is the traditional description of the ideogram , this one and others like it should probably be regarded as representing daggers.

2. se–to –i – ja   wa – na – ka – te– ra   cloth 40 wool 100

† See Appendix One

3

This tablet is from the cloth and wool inventories at Knossos. The word on the left is the name of the place where the wool was worked. The record probably notes consignments of wool which are to be made into pieces of cloth. wa–na–ka = ϝάναζ (lord). wa–na–ka–te–ra, which is used in this inscription, is a neuter plural adjective probably meaning 'fit for the lord'.

3. 

a – ke – ti ri – ja woman 12 ko–wa 16 ko-wo 8 DA 1TA1

This is one of a group of tablets found at Pylos giving numbers of women, boys and girls as part of a census. a–ke–ti–ri–ja could mean decorators or finishers. ko–wa = κόρϝαι (girls) and ko–wo = κόρϝοι (boys). Therefore, the text states that twelve women 'decorators' form a group together with sixteen girls and eight boys. DA is thought to represent a male supervisor and TA a female supervisor.

The women mentioned are probably slaves organised into work units. In other inscriptions in the same collection are the feminine nouns ki–ni–di–ja (of Knidos) and mi–ra–ti–ja (of Miletus), possibly denoting the place of origin of the women.

The place name pu–ro (Pylos) is found on some tablets and on another there is a mention of wheat and figs which may have served as rations for the workers.

Some elements of Mycenaean which had fallen out of use by the eighth century BC give us valuable information for the reconstruction of early Greek. The w or v sound represented by digamma in the Greek alphabet was partially known from certain dialects but it is found in full use in Mycenaean Greek, e.g. genitive singular di–wo = ΔιϝόϚ cf. Att. ΔιόϚ (of Zeus), wi–de = ϝίδε cf. Att. εἶδε (he saw) and wa–na–ka = ϝάναξ cf. Att. ἄναξ (lord). The Indo-European k^w group of sounds has not yet undergone a transformation to π or τ, nor has the g^w group of sounds yet changed to β or δ. Therefore, in Linear B the forms e–qe–ta, –qe and qa–si–re–u are found, corresponding to the Attic forms ἐπέτᾱϚ (follower), τε (and) and βασιλεύϚ (king). It is also interesting to compare the early Indo-European forms illustrated above with some equivalents in Latin, such as Iovis, video, sequor and –que.

It would be rash to claim that we know how the Mycenaeans spoke and there must have been dialect differences within Mycenaean Greek itself which are not revealed in Linear B. Apart from the linguistic interest of the inscriptions, however, there is a fascinating wealth of information about social and administrative matters. We are given such details as lists of place names and weapons, a census of animals, inventories of cloth, wheels and chariots, records of people engaged in various activities including military dispositions and assessments of commodities. For example, we learn that in Pylos and Tiryns the size of a land-holding was measured by productivity or yield rather than by its area. Religious texts give evidence for the use of oil in worship and indicate the types of offerings made. Large numbers of sheep are mentioned in the Knossos tablets suggesting that there was a flourishing wool industry in Crete at this time.

All in all we are given a tantalising glimpse into a past age. With regard to our knowledge of the Greek language, we learn that it was in use from, at the latest, the fourteenth century BC in Crete and probably earlier on the mainland. Linear B inscriptions have also been found on clay vases in a number of mainland sites and their dates fall within the fourteenth and fifteenth centuries.

Until the decipherment of Linear B the earliest evidence for Greek had been an inscription on a wine jar found in the Kerameikos cemetery area of Athens and this dated back only to the eighth century BC. Therefore, in the words of J. Chadwick, it can truly be said that the discovery of Linear B 'pushed back some seven centuries the date of the earliest Greek inscriptions, and this extended our knowledge of the Greek language, which now has a continuous recorded history totalling thirty-three centuries, a record rivalled only by the Chinese'.[3]

This detailed evidence for the fourteenth and thirteenth centuries BC in Greece must be set in the context of the history of both the country and the language. There are signs of human habitation in Greece dating back to 40,000 BC or earlier. Farming communities on the Greek mainland can be identified as far back as the seventh millenium and by 6000 BC obsidian from Melos was found over a wide area. Painted pottery, clay and stone figurines, tools and weapons have been found at mainland sites from the fifth and fourth millenia and by the early Bronze Age (third millenium) there were movements of people of a similar level of civilisation in an area comprising mainland Greece, the islands of the Aegean, Crete, Cyprus and Asia Minor. Three separate cultures have been identified for the Aegean area in the Bronze Age and these are conventionally called the Cycladic, Minoan and Helladic cultures.

The Cycladic culture, which does not directly concern us here, developed in the Aegean islands round Delos. The Minoan culture takes its name from the term used by Sir Arthur Evans recalling the legendary King Minos of Knossos. This civilisation was centred on Crete and reached its height in power and wealth during the years from 2000 BC to 1550 BC. Its splendour can be judged from what has remained of the great palaces at Knossos, Phaistos, Mallia and Zakro and from the many artefacts which have been found not only throughout Crete but on the Greek mainland, on many Aegean islands and in Syria, Palestine and Egypt. In fact, from everything that is known about these people, such as their elaborate but functional style of architecture, the vitality of their art and the organisation of their society, we gain the impression that they were outstandingly peace-loving and prosperous. Unfortunately, we do not know their language, for the pictographic and Linear A scripts, which are thought to represent it, have yet to be deciphered. The Minoans were not Greeks and they may have been related to other Indo-European peoples of Asia Minor. Nevertheless, they came to have a profound influence on the subsequent character of Greek culture as will be shown.

During the same period as that of the supremacy of the Minoans in Crete, we have evidence for the appearance of the first Greek-speaking peoples on the mainland. No one can say for certain when they came or from where. The earlier mainland culture of the third millenium BC conventionally referred to as Early Helladic, had suffered a period of destruction and decline and it was possible that newcomers of Greek stock were establishing themselves during the transitional period of 2200 to 1900 BC. Whatever their origins, these new people developed into an agricultural community and produced a distinctive style of pottery which has been given the name of Minyan ware. Their level of civilisation, however, was lower than that of their mainland predecessors and the extent of their trade overseas was limited compared with that of the Minoans.

Some time after this, however, Minoan influence began to make itself felt on the mainland. For example, burial gifts found in the Shaft Graves at Mycenae which date back to the sixteenth century BC reveal a sudden access of wealth and have certain Minoan characteristics combined with Helladic elements. Some objects which were found are purely Cretan, such as a silver rhyton in the shape of a bull's head with gold horns, others are purely Helladic, such as the gold funeral masks. The bronze swords and dagger blades, on the other hand, which are decorated with hunting scenes in gold, silver and niello, inlaid into the smooth surface, are a combination of characteristics of both cultures. This fusion of cultures, which is so interesting, marks the beginning of the civilisation known as

Mycenaean and it must have been at this time that the Linear B script began to be used.

During the sixteenth and early fifteenth centuries both Crete and the mainland of Greece prospered but after 1450 BC there was considerable destruction of sites on Crete. The cause of this remains in dispute, the possibilities being rebellion, a Mycenaean invasion or a volcanic eruption, the latter being the most likely. On the mainland, however, Mycenae entered upon a period of rapid expansion and became the dominant city in the Argolid. Other palace centres were established at Tiryns, Pylos, Thebes, Orchomenos, Volos, Gla (in Boeotia) and Athens. The connections between Mycenae and Crete during this period are not wholly clear but Linear B tablets found in Knossos dating back to the destruction of the palace in the fourteenth century indicate that the Greek language was in use there. We do not know for certain, however, whether mainlanders took control at Knossos or whether the Minoans themselves had started to use Greek for their own official purposes.

The Mycenaeans seem to have been a more warlike people than the Minoans. Their palaces were strongly fortified with massive monumental gates such as the Lion Gate at Mycenae. Their more warlike view of life can also be detected in illustrations of a military character which are seen in Mycenaean art. For example, a vase of the thirteenth century BC, known as the Warrior Vase, shows six warriors, fully-armed, leaving for war. If all this indicates that the rulers felt insecure there may have been good reason for their fears, for by 1200 BC many of the mainland sites had been destroyed.

There is clear evidence for destruction and decline in the Mycenaean world at this time but, just as with the end of the Minoan civilisation, we do not know the causes. Old theories suggested an invasion of Doric speaking Greeks from the North-West but an alternative theory is that speakers of the Doric dialect were already present in the Mycenaean world but are unknown to us because their dialect, not being official, was not used for the official records. In accordance with this theory, the disturbances which brought about the downfall of the palaces could have been a result of an uprising of the mass of the population against their rulers. Whatever the reason was, the palaces lost their power and Linear B fell out of use, leaving us with no written evidence for the state of the Greek language for the next four centuries.

This period is often referred to as the Dark Age of Greece but, in fact, even without written records, we know much more about it than that title implies. It was during this period that the Greeks established colonies in

7

Italy and on the Asia Minor coast. Contact between Greece and the Near East, especially Phoenicia, led to the establishment of permanent trading posts in the Near East and trade routes stretched between there and the new colonies in western Italy. At home, communities had become isolated and developed independently, city-states grew up, a new hoplite class emerged within the predominantly aristocratic society and there was the phenomenon of tyranny. Moves towards democracy in Athens began with the codification of laws and Kleisthenes' reforms, at the end of the sixth century BC, led to the participative democracy of Athens. Other city-states developed different types of political system but all were, nevertheless, linked by their shared religion, customs and language.

The Near East connection brought Greece not only new styles of pottery and new ideas but also an alphabet. The introduction of a Phoenician style of alphabet which could be readily adapted to the Greek language led to the re-emergence of the art of writing in Greece, this time with a high degree of flexibility. The earliest inscription which we possess in this new alphabetic script is a wine-jar inscription from the Dipylon cemetery in Athens dated to approximately 750 BC. The inscription is incised on the shoulder of the jar and proclaims that it is, 'a prize for whichever of the dancers dances best':

ὃς νῦν ὀρχηστῶν πάντων ἀταλώτατα παίζει το(ῦ)το δεκᾶν μιν.

(The explanation of δεκᾶν as δέχεσθαι, however, is doubtful.)

One possible explanation for the introduction of this alphabet is that it was learnt and adapted by Greeks who traded with Phoenicia, possibly Greeks who actually lived in the Syro-Phoenician area. The script chosen was the North Semitic one and consisted of twenty-two characters but no vowel signs. The Greeks adapted this by using certain signs whose sounds did not exist in Greek to represent the missing vowels. The result was a Greek alphabet retaining the order and names of the Phoenician characters without, however, giving any significance to the names.†

The new Greek alphabet soon developed a number of local variations. A West Greek version, used in Italy and Sicily, was the predecessor of the alphabet of the Romans. On the mainland of Greece the East Ionic alphabet became the standard form by the end of the fifth century BC but before this time long e was not distinguished from short e, and the

† See Appendix Two

diphthong ou and long o were not distinguished from short o. An example of the earlier form can be seen in the following inscription on an Athenian cup dating to the middle of the seventh century BC:

θαρίο εἰμί ποτέριον
(ου)   (η)

I am the drinking cup of Tharius

Two further aspects of classical Greek remain to be discussed, its Indo-European origin and its division into dialects.

The earliest evidence for the Indo-European family of languages dates back to the second millenium BC and the Greek Linear B tablets are the second oldest inscriptions that we possess, being preceded by Hittite inscriptions and followed by those in Sanskrit. From comparative evidence original Indo-European can be seen to have been an inflected language and the Indo-European languages share many correspondences in declensions and conjugations. Many 'common' words are similar, such as those for pronouns, numbers and family relationships.† All this is fully evident in the Greek language which, as we have seen, was probably brought into the Balkan peninsula at the beginning of the second millenium BC.

In the vocabulary of Greek, however, there are also words belonging to an earlier stratum. For example, for *sea* the Indo-European languages generally use words from the IE root *mori* (cf. Latin *mare*, German *meer*) whereas the Greeks use words such as ἅλς, πόντος, πέλαγος and θάλασσα, the last having the –σσα ending which is characteristic of several pre-Greek place names. Many place names belonging to an older language end in –σσος (–ττος) or –νθος, such as Παρνασσός, Λάρισ(σ)α, Ὑμηττός, Κόρινθος and Ζάκυνθος. Other pre-Greek words include ἀσάμινθος bath-tub, θάλαμος inner part of house, πύργος tower and μέγαρον large room or house, words which indicate the high standard of living already mentioned in connection with the Early Helladic period. The identity of these pre-Greeks is not known, but, as in the case of the peoples of Minoan Crete and the Cyclades, a connection with the Anatolian area of Asia Minor is likely, especially since place-names

---

† See Appendix Three

* The asterisk is used here to denote a reconstructed word and it will be used in this way throughout the rest of this chapter.

with similar endings were found in Asia Minor such as Telmessos, Halicarnassos, Assos, Lindos and Aspendos. Memories of pre-Greek inhabitants are found among the ancient Greeks themselves in tales such as that of Herodotus who suggests that the Athenians were descended from an earlier stock whom he calls Pelasgian and who, he says, 'changed their language when they were absorbed into the Greek family of nations'.[4] Whether pre-Greek was an Indo-European language or not is still a matter of debate among scholars.[5]

Lacking documentary evidence, we cannot trace the details of the development of the language in Greece for its first thousand years, but by the eighth century BC we find that a variety of local dialects are already well established. The geographical spread of the dialects reflects the movements that took place after the fall of the Mycenaean civilisation when numbers of people migrated either to settle in other parts of Greece or to set up colonies overseas. The different dialects which developed in the spoken language are usually divided into four main groups.

Arcado-Cypriot, with such features as σις for τις, κάς for καί and a 3rd person middle ending in –τοι, was spoken in the central Peloponnese and in Cyprus. One theory for the isolation of Arcadian in the centre of the Peloponnese is that the speakers of this dialect were driven inland from the coastal areas by the Dorian conquerors and one theory for the Cypriot connection is that the island was colonised from the Peloponnese before this event.

The dialect group which we know as West Greek because of its location before the migrations had a Doric branch found in the southern and eastern parts of the Peloponnese, in Crete and in a small area of coastal Asia Minor and a North-West Greek branch, found in the northwestern Peloponnese and north of the Gulf of Corinth. Characteristics of Doric include many archaic features such as the retention of original τ in such forms as δίδωτι for δίδωσι, Ποτειδάν for Ποσειδῶν, τριακάτιοι for τριακόσιοι and the article forms τοί, ταί for οἱ, αἱ. ποτί is found for πρός, πόκα for πότε, φέρομες for φέρομεν and τῆνος for ἐκεῖνος.

Ionic was spoken in Asia Minor from Halicarnassos to Smyrna and in the Cyclades and Euboea. The language of Athens, Attic, was closely related to it and the whole group is known as Attic-Ionic. In this dialect original ᾱ became ε̄, as in δῆμος and μήτηρ for δᾶμος and μάτηρ. The personal pronouns have the forms ἡμέες/ἡμεῖς and ἡμέας/ἡμᾶς whereas the other dialects show forms such as ἀμές/ἀμέ or ἄμμες/ἄμμε. It should be noted, however, that by a further development the change from ᾱ to ε̄ in the Attic dialect was inhibited after ε, ι and ρ, as in the examples οἰκία and θύρα.

In both Attic and Ionic α + ο appears as εω whereas in other dialects it appears as āo or ā. For example, λαϝός (people) in most dialects is λᾱός but in Attic-Ionic it is λεώς. Similarly νεώς (temple) is found instead of νᾱός.

Certain combinations of consonants develop to σσ in Ionic but to ττ in Attic, as in θάλασσα (Ionic) and θάλαττα (Attic). Ionic does not contract εα and εο whereas Attic does, as in the genitive singular of γένος, where the Ionic form is γένεος and the Attic form is γένους.

In spite of some differences, however, the two forms are usually classed as one group and it is this dialect of the Greek language which looks the most familiar to us of all the Greek dialects, the reason being that this is the dialect which was to become the basis of the common Greek language as it was established at the end of the fourth century BC.

The fourth main dialect was known as Aeolic and was spoken from Smyrna northwards to the Hellespont, in Thessaly and in Boeotia. In the two latter areas, however, the language also contained several Doric elements. Some special features of Aeolic are the representation of some labiovelars as π, as in πέσσαρες for τέσσαρες or πῆλε for τῆλε, and third declension dative plurals ending in -εσσι.[6]

These were the main dialects of spoken Greek but there were also special literary dialects and each type of literature had its own character-istic one. This was usually the dialect of the area in which that particular genre had developed and once this identification had been established all later writers used the appropriate dialect, regardless of their own native tongue. Boeotian Hesiod, for example, did not write in Aeolic but in the dialect of epic poetry. This particular literary dialect was unique in that it did not belong to any one place or time but was an amalgam of forms resulting from a varied oral tradition. The area in which it arose was Ionian Greece and it is often referred to as the Homeric dialect. It con-tained elements of Aeolic as well as the predominant Ionic forms and it was a dialect which no-one spoke but which was so familiar to all Greeks that its forms were used in epic poetry for many centuries. Lyric poetry was composed during the same early period as the works of Homer and some of the lyric poets also used the Homeric dialect. For choral lyric, however, which developed in Sparta under Alcman, Doric became the conventional dialect and this dialect was used both by Pindar, who was a Boeotian, and Simonides and Bacchylides who were Ionians. Ionic was the dialect of philosophy, of the histories of the sixth century BC and of Herodotus, while Attic became established as the language of drama.

Attic was also used by Thucydides in prose towards the end of the fifth century BC and this set the pattern for the Attic dialect being accepted from that time on as the language of literary prose. By the fourth century BC the use of Attic was widespread.

When we speak of the literature of ancient Greece, we generally mean the writings of the seventh to the fourth centuries BC. Because so much of this literature has been preserved, we are able to gain from it a clear understanding of the language of the ancient Greeks. Although it is a literary language and not necessarily the same as the spoken one, we assume that it was accessible to all Greeks and we can see that most of its main features have been retained in all subsequent developments of the language. For the history of the classical period and the study of its literature, I refer the reader elsewhere. Certain standard works are listed in the bibliography.

Analytical studies of the Greek language were first made by the Stoics in the third century BC and at the same time, in Alexandria, many scholars were busy storing and putting in order classical texts. This involved such aids as the addition of punctuation, a standardisation of the alphabet and possibly accentuation, although there is no full use of the system of accents with which we are familiar until the ninth century AD. In connection with this kind of scholarship, grammatical definitions were established but the only extant book which we possess on this subject is a small volume called 'Τέχνη Γραμματική' written by Dionysius Thrax during the second century BC. He was a native of Alexandria who taught in Rhodes and his book was intended to describe 'what was for the most part being said by poets and prose-writers'. He defined eight parts of speech and summarised the different types of grammatical study which must have been well-known by his time, using terminology which is recognisable in all later Greek grammars.

As an inflected language, ancient Greek expressed its grammatical relationships by means of different endings. Every inflected word has a fundamental part called a 'stem', a development of an earlier 'root', to which are added endings and sometimes prefixes, to indicate case, tense, person and voice.

e.g.

12

ά	θ α ν	α	τ ο	ς
	root	suf-		
prefix	θ–ν		fix	ending
	STEM			

Nouns, adjectives and pronouns all decline but Greek uses less 'cases' than other Indo-European languages, the functions of ablative, locative and instrument being absorbed by the genitive and dative cases. The dual number, originally used for things going in pairs, remained common in Attic Greek but generally became increasingly rare except in poetry.

The ancient Greek verb has three basic tense groupings which are formed by the modification of its stem. For example, λύω—I loose has three forms: λυ—present, λυσ—future/aorist and λελυκ—perfect. The stem often undergoes a change of vowel such as in λείπω—I leave which has the forms λειπ–, λιπ– and λελοιπ–. This is a characteristic feature of Indo-European languages and a similar type of change is seen in the English 'sing, sang, sung'.

Prepositions were formed from adverbs and were often associated with verbs to form compounds. Particles such as τε, δέ, μέν...δέ and δή connected one sentence to the preceding one or indicated a balance within a short or long period.

Changes within words were made to avoid displeasing sounds and so in Attic Greek τιμάω is changed to τιμῶ. Such changes as that of ἔδωκε ἐκεῖνο to ἔδωκεν ἐκεῖνο and *πάντσι to πᾶσι were made for the same reason. The sentence as a whole had a musical quality and one which would be unfamiliar to our ears, since two different types of accentuation were present. The accent of each word indicated pitch rather than stress, the word for accent—τόνος—literally meaning 'a stretching of the strings'. In addition to this pitch accent, however, each word also bore a stress on the last heavy syllable.

e.g.   ἄνθρωπος   πάρεστι
        ἄνθρωπος   ἔρχεται

The general rules of syntax in ancient Greek are familiar to speakers of Indo-European languages and only a few special points need be mentioned. In Indirect Statements both the infinitive and ὅτι or ὡς followed by the indicative or the optative are found. After verbs expressing perception a participle is used, as in ἤκουσε Κῦρον ἐν Κιλικίᾳ ὄντα. A noun and a participle not connected with the main construction of the sentence stand by themselves in the genitive case (genitive absolute) and there is also an 'accusative absolute' for participles of impersonal verbs, such as δέον (it being necessary). The tenses of the indicative mark the notion of time but the tenses of the subjunctive and imperative, and the optative and infinitive when not in indirect statement, differ in aspect rather than in time. The present denotes a continued or repeated action, while the aorist denotes a simple occurrence of the action, a distinction which is found today in modern Greek and also in Russian. One characteristic of ancient Greek which was later lost is the use of a singular verb after a neuter plural subject. This is an Indo-European usage in which the plurals must originally have been thought of as collective nouns.

By the end of the fourth century BC, following the conquests of Alexander the Great, Greek was beginning to be accepted as the common tongue of an empire which covered the whole of the eastern Mediterranean, Egypt, Syria, Mesopotamia and Iran. Greek memories even lingered on further east in Afghanistan and India. The spread of Greek civilisation was not just a result of conquest but was also the result of extensive colonisation. New cities were founded in the east and the Greeks who inhabited them came from many different areas of their former Greek homeland. It was inevitable, therefore, that the ancient dialects would have to give way to a language that would be common to all Greeks. This was the κοινὴ διάλεκτος (common language) which was based on the Attic dialect of Athens as it had been adapted by Philip II of Macedon in the mid-fourth century BC.

The development and use of this new form of the language will form the subject of the rest of this book. The main aim is to show that there is a continuity and that the modern language is remarkably close to its ancient ancestor.

CHAPTER TWO

THE BEGINNINGS OF MODERN GREEK—
THE COMMON DIALECT (Η ΚΟΙΝΗ ΔΙΑΛΕΚΤΟΣ)
THIRD CENTURY BC–ELEVENTH CENTURY AD

By the third century BC Greek was the official language of the new cities of the Eastern Mediterranean and it was adopted by many people for whom it was not their native tongue. The Jews of Alexandria, for example, became Greek-speaking and eventually the Hebrew scriptures were translated into Greek for their use. This Greek translation of the Old Testament, known as the Septuagint because it was said to have been translated by seventy rabbis, is now one of our sources for Hellenistic Greek. Other sources for this common language, the Koine, are listed by Robert Browning in his book *Medieval and Modern Greek*.[7] Among them are literary texts, such as the Histories of Polybius and Diodorus and the Discourses of Epictetus, the New Testament and certain other early Christian writings, a mass of letters and documents surviving on papyrus and the observations of grammarians. This last group has already been mentioned and, out of the others, extracts will be given later in this chapter from the New Testament, early Christian literature and letters found on papyri. All of these will give an idea of the form of the spoken language.

By the end of the first century BC the whole of the Hellenistic world was under the rule of the Romans but the Greek language still predominated in this area; official documents, for example, were produced in Greek as well as Latin. The Romans made the study of Greek literature an integral part of their education programme and the highest stage of education was entirely Greek in character. Attendance at Athens university would be the culmination of many an upper-class Roman boy's studies.

Ancient Greece can be said to have come to an end with the burning of Athens by the Heruli in the third century AD but by that time a new influence was already gaining a hold on the peoples of the Greek world.

15

This was Christianity which was supplanting many of the pagan religions. Its most active centres in its early years were in Asia Minor, Syria and Egypt. It soon spread through the rest of the Greek-speaking part of the Empire and almost all the early Christians knew Greek. In North Africa, Asia Minor and Southern Europe, Greek would have been used by Christian preachers and it was naturally the language of the earliest Christian literature, such as the Gospels, the letters of St Paul and the writings of the Fathers of the Church. It is through the Church, in fact, that the common dialect of those early centuries, ἡ κοινὴ διάλεκτος, is preserved today, for during the first five hundred years of Christian worship a set liturgy developed which is still sung in the Greek Orthodox Church in its original form. The word λειτουργία originally meant a public service or duty and for Orthodox Christians this is the duty of sharing in the prayers, hymns and gospel readings throughout the year. This liturgical custom was one of the ways in which the Greek language managed to survive the later centuries of foreign rule.

Eventually the Greek, Roman and Christian influences were all to come together in one city, Constantinople. The Emperor Constantine transferred the capital of the Roman Empire there in the fourth century AD and made Christianity the Empire's official religion. Although Latin continued to be used for formal purposes at first, it was Greek that predominated in every other aspect of life. In the sixth century AD Greek became the official language of the independent empire which had developed around Constantinople, the Eastern Roman or Byzantine Empire.

One of the main differences between the new κοινὴ διάλεκτος and ancient Greek was a change in pronunciation which affected not only the sound of words but eventually their appearance as well. An understanding of the pronunciation changes and their effect on orthography will immediately throw light on the meaning of many unfamiliar-looking words in modern Greek. A summary of the pronunciation of modern Greek is given in Appendix Four. Another major difference was that the new dialect went through a process of simplification to suit the great variety of peoples who were then using it.

The early development of the modern Greek language is very well illustrated in letters and documents surviving on papyri, most of which have been found in Egypt and which show the use of Greek by ordinary people for personal or business purposes. The New Testament, on the other hand, and the religious poetry of the period give us a more correct written version of the κοινὴ διάλεκτος; pronunciation changes are not apparent but the vocabulary and simple style cannot have been too far removed from everyday speech.

Errors in spelling in the Egyptian papyri are a good indication of the changes in pronunciation, as in the following short extract found at Oxyrhynchus dating from the first century AD:

Ἡρακληείδης Ἀσκλατᾶι χαίρειν. δὸς τῶ κομείζοντί σου τὴν ἐπιστολὴν τὴν λαογραφίαν Μνησιθέου καὶ τὸ ναύβιον, καὶ πέμψον ἡμεῖν περὶ τῶν βιβλίον ἧ ἐξήρτισας.

Heraclides to Asclatas, greeting. Give the bearer of this letter the poll-tax of Mnesitheus and the 'naubion', and send me word about the documents, how you have completed them.[8]

(The 'naubion' was a duty concerned with the building or repair of dykes or houses.) κομείζοντι and ἡμεῖν show that the pronunciation of ει is identical to that of ι (κομίζοντι, ἡμῖν). τῶν βιβλίον for τῶν βιβλίων shows the identification of the sounds o and ω.

Some of the major changes of pronunciation, which remain to this day, are:

i) the loss of a distinction between long and short vowels; all simple vowels being short.

e.g. ω has the same sound as o

ii) ι, η, οι and ει being pronounced as ι

(Later υ and υι took the same pronunciation, leading to the predominance of the i sound in modern Greek.)

iii) αι being pronounced as ε

iv) αυ being pronounced as af *or* av, and ευ as ef *or* ev

v) ζ being pronounced as z (not dz)

vi) voiced and aspirated plosives becoming spirants

e.g. β → v φ(pʰ) → ph

γ → gh χ(cʰ) → ch (lo<u>ch</u>)

δ → th (<u>then</u>) θ(tʰ) → th (<u>think</u>)

vii) the loss of the second element of long diphthongs, traditionally shown as an iota subscript

viii) the loss of the force of the rough breathing

ix) the accent changing from indicating the pitch of the voice to indicating the stress on the word.

A similar process of simplification is also apparent in the reduction of the inflected forms of words. In nouns, pronouns and adjectives the use of the genitive was restricted and the use of the dative was lost except for certain set phrases, such as δόξα τῷ Θεῷ. In both nouns and verbs the dual number fell out of use. Some details of the changes which are believed to have occurred during this period are given below:

Nouns

i) First declension nouns kept the same vowel in all cases:

	nominative	accusative	genitive
e.g.	ὁ ναύτης	τὸν ναύτην	τοῦ ναύτῃ
	ἡ θάλασσα	τὴν θάλασσαν	τῆς θαλάσσας

ii) In first declension nouns the plural ending –αι, on the analogy of third declension plurals, seemed to lack a ς, and was changed to –ες. Also, by the first century AD, the accusative plural of the third declension nouns had begun to show the same ending as the nominative, and this tendency spread to the first declension. The result of all this was the simplification of the first declension endings as follows:

	singular	plural
nominative	–α –η –ας –ης	–ες
accusative	–αν –ην –αν –ην	–ες
genitive	–ας –ης –α –η	–ων

iii) In the third declension, the accusative ending in –α seemed incomplete in comparison with the first and second declension ending –ν and this led to an interesting series of changes.

e.g. τὸν πατέρα changed to τὸν πατέραν and τὴν ἐλπίδα to τὴν ἐλπίδαν.

Then, because the new accusative resembled the first declension, a new nominative of a first-declension type was used, so that ὁ πατήρ became ὁ πατέρας and ἡ ἐλπίς became ἡ ἐλπίδα and the singular declined as follows:

	accusative	genitive
nominative		
ὁ πατέρας	τὸν πατέραν	τοῦ πατέρα
ἡ ἐλπίδα	τὴν ἐλπίδαν	τῆς ἐλπίδας

iv) The second declension nouns, such as ὁ ἄγγελος, preserved their basic form intact.

The result of these modifications was the loss of a distinctive third declension. An explanation of the modern Greek categorisation of nouns into two declensions is given in the next chapter when further changes of ending and the loss of final –ν in the accusative singular are discussed (pages 42–3).

Pronouns

i) By analogy with the forms of ἐγώ and ἡμεῖς, ἐσέ and ἐσού were created in the singular and ἐσεῖς replaced ὑμεῖς as the second person plural. These changes were followed by further developments of the accusative singular of each pronoun. First they acquired a final –ν, and then –αν to assimilate them to nouns. With time the final –ν fell out of use.

e.g. ἐγώ   ἐσύ
   ἐμέ → ἐμέν → ἐμένα(ν)   ἐσέ → ἐσέν → ἐσένα(ν)
   ἐμοῦ   ἐσοῦ
   ἡμεῖς   ἐσεῖς
   ἡμᾶς   ἐσᾶς
   ἡμῶν   ἐσῶν

ii) The pronoun οὗτος caused difficulty because of its changes of stem and was simplified to τοῦτος τούτη τοῦτο. It was also sometimes written as ἐτοῦτος on analogy with ἐκεῖνος which remained in use.

Verbs

The number of different verb forms was reduced. Strong aorists were eliminated, irregular forms were assimilated to regular, the perfect tense began to be merged with the aorist and the optative and the dual fell out of use. Middle aorists were replaced by passive forms and, in effect, the three voices of ancient Greek were reduced to two, active and medio-passive. The four moods of ancient Greek were reduced to three: indicative, subjunctive and imperative.

e.g. ἔφυγον → ἔφυγα
   –μι verbs → –ω e.g. δείκνυμι → δείκνω
   ἐσκεψάμην → ἐσκέφθην

Verb stems were simplified to a present and aorist stem as in φευγ– and φυγ–, and these stems were used to express different aspects rather than tenses. From the present stem were formed the present and past tenses of the indefinite, or incomplete, aspect, as 'I go, I am going, I was going'. From the aorist stem was formed the past tense of definitive, or completed, aspect, as 'I went'. These two stems each formed its own imperative and subjunctive with the same distinction of aspect. This distinction was already present in these moods in ancient Greek, as in:

εὖ γράφε—write well (whenever you write)

τοῦτο γράψον—write this (now, i.e. definite).

The old future tense did not fit into the new system of two aspects and, after changes in pronunciation, it could also have been confused with the aorist subjunctive. It, therefore, began to be replaced by a series of periphrases, such as θέλω νὰ γράψω. These will be described in greater detail in the next chapter (pages 59–60).

The tendency to express more fully in words a meaning which would have been expressed by inflection in ancient Greek can also be seen today in the periphrastic forms of the perfect and pluperfect tenses (ἔχω γράψει, εἶχα γράψει) which will be discussed later (pages 70–1).

The following changes occurred early:

i) The endings of the imperfect and aorist tenses were simplified and followed the same system:

	singular	plural
1	–α	–αμεν
2	–ες	–ατε
3	–ε	–αν

ii) The aorist imperative was simplified on analogy with the present imperative:

γράψον → γράψε

iii) The second person singular of the present passive was brought into line with the other passive endings:

1	λέγομαι
2	λέγεσαι (instead of λέγει)
3	λέγεται

iv) A new form of the third person plural of the present tense developed, ending in –ουν, although the –ουσι form survived for a long time and both forms were often used by the same writer.

The reduction in the number of inflections may have been one of the reasons for the change in style which also occurred during this period.

The carefully-constructed periods of ancient Greek, in which a main verb was accompanied by several subordinate clauses and participial phrases, gave way to a more co-ordinated style in which several main verbs were joined together by conjunctions. This style is evident in the New Testament where it may also have been influenced by the similar style of Semitic writing. At the same time, the reduction in the number of cases led to an increase in the number and use of prepositions.

Vocabulary changes also occurred, attributable to both internal and external causes. One external influence was that of Christianity, which brought such new meanings to words as that of 'church' to ἐκκλησία (assembly) and that of 'angel' to ἄγγελος (messenger). New words deriving from Hebrew included Πάσχα (Easter—The Passover) and Σάββατο (Saturday—the Sabbath). From Latin came κῆνσος (census) and ὁσπίτιον (hospitium—poor house, lodging), which today is simplified to σπίτι (a house). Other examples of new meanings attached to old words are ὀψάριον (a delicacy) which was also used for 'fish' and is used with that meaning in the simplified modern form of it, ψάρι, and φθάνω (I anticipate) which also came to mean 'I arrive'.

One type of internal change was the replacement of certain irregular nouns with synonyms which were better suited to the new simple noun forms. For example, ναῦς—ship (ἡ ναῦς τῆς νεώς) was replaced by τὸ πλοῖον, οὖς—ear (τὸ οὖς τοῦ ὠτός) by τὸ ὠτίον (later αὐτί) and ὕδωρ—water (τὸ ὕδωρ τοῦ ὕδατος) by τὸ νεαρόν (fresh i.e. fresh water) which is today used in the simplified form of νερό.

In the extracts which follow the changes in style and vocabulary are more evident than the grammatical simplifications. Even in the literature which approximated more closely to everyday speech there remained a certain formality which maintained many of the traditional forms of grammar. This fact, however, means that the study of the literature of this period can be readily accessible to any student of ancient Greek. An understanding of the processes of simplification outlined in this chapter combined with a knowledge of the basic features of ancient Greek can then lead on to an appreciation of later Greek literature and the form of the Greek language which is spoken today. Modern Greek has both stability and flexibility, and it owes this to its long history. Modern writers may base their themes on twentieth century experiences but the inspiration of many of them will inevitably be drawn from the past as well. Just as no true appreciation of modern Greece can be gained without an understanding of its history, so there can be no true appreciation of its literature without an understanding of the rich linguistic and cultural heritage which lies behind it.

Papyri

1. 2nd century AD. Antonius Longus writes to his mother. It seems that his irregular mode of life has caused a rift between himself and his mother and he has left home. Now he repents and pleads for reconciliation. The letter is not complete.

'Αντῶνις Λόγγος Νειλοῦτι τῇ μητρί πλῖστα χαίρειν. Καὶ διὰ πάντων εὔχομαί σαι ὑγειαίνειν. Τὸ προσκύνημά σου ποιῶ κατ' αἰκάστην ἡμαίραν παρὰ τω κυρίω Σεραπείδει. Γεινώσκειν σαι θέλω, ὅτι οὐχ ἤλπιζον, ὅτι ἀναβένις εἰς τὴν μητρόπολιν. Χάρειν τοῦτο οὐδ' ἐγὸ εἰσῆλθα εἰς τὴν πόλιν. Αἰδυσοπούμην δὲ ἐλθεῖν εἰς Καρανίδαν, ὅτι σαπρῶς παιριπατῶ. Αἴγραψά σοι, ὅτι γυμνός εἰμαι. Παρακαλῶ σαι, μήτηρ, διαλάγητί μοι. Λοιπόν, οἶδα τίποτ' αἰμαυτω παρέσχημαι. παιπαίδευμαι, καθ' ὃν δῖ τρόπον. Οἶδα ὅτι ἡμάρτηκα. Ἤκουσα παρὰ τοῦ Ποστούμου τὸν εὑρόντα σαι ἐν τω Ἀρσαινοείτῃ, καὶ ἀκαίρως πάντα σοι διήγηται. Οὐκ οἶδες, ὅτι θέλω πηρὸς γενέσται εἰ γνοῦναι, ὅπως ἀνθρόπω ἔτι ὀφείλω ὀβολόν;
Νειλοῦτι μητρεὶ ἀπ' Ἀντωνίω Λόγγου νειοῦ.

(B.G.U. 846)

Antonius Longus to Nilous his mother very many greetings. I pray always for your health; every day I make supplication for you before the Lord Serapis. I would have you know that I did not expect that you were going up to the metropolis (*Arsinoe, capital of nome*); for that reason I did not come to the city myself. I was ashamed to come to Karanis (*village in Fayum, home of writer's mother*) because I go about in filth. I wrote to you that I am naked. I beg you, mother, be reconciled to me. Well, I know what I have brought on myself. I have received a fitting lesson. I know that I have sinned. I heard from…who found you in the Arsinoite nome, and he has told you everything correctly. Do you not know that I would rather be maimed than feel that I still owe a man an obol?…
(Addressed) to Nilous his mother from Antonius Longus her son.[9]

Note the absence of the iota subscript as in τῶ κυρίω, τῇ (μητρί) and the following changes in pronunciation:

ει pronounced as ι	πλῖστα = πλεῖστα, χάρειν = χάριν
αι pronounced as ε	αἱκάστην = ἑκάστην, σαι = σε
ω pronounced as ο	ἐγό = ἐγώ, ἀνθρόπω = ἀνθρώπῳ
η pronounced as ι	δῖ = δῆ

κατ᾽ αἱκάστην instead of καθ᾽ αἱκάστην indicates the loss of the rough breathing, and a reverse mistake can be seen in οὐχ ἤλπιζον where the χ presupposes a subsequent rough breathing, which did not exist.

2. 2nd or 3rd century AD. Serenilla is alone in Alexandria and waiting for her father to write to her.

Σερηνίλλα Σωκράτη τῶ πατρὶ πλῖστα χαίρειν. Πρὸ μὲν πάντων εὔχομαί σαι ὑγιαίνιν καὶ τὸ προσκύνημά σου ποιῶ κατ᾽ ἐκάστην ἡμέραν παρὰ τῶ κυρίω Σαράπιδι καὶ τοῖς συννέοις θεοῖς. Γεινώσκειν σε θέλω, ὅτι μόνη ἱμὶ ἐγώ. Ἐν νόω ἔχης ὅτι ἡ θυγάτηρ μου ἰς Ἀλεξάνδρειαν ἔσσι, ἵνα καἰγὼ εἰδῶ, ὅτι πατέρα ἔχω, εἴνα μὴ ἴδωσείν με ὡς μὴ ἔχουσαν γονεῖς. Καὶ ὁ ἐνιγών σοι τὴν ἐπιστολὴν δὸς αὐτῶ ἄλλην περὶ τῆς ὑίας σου. Καὶ ἀσπάζομαι τὴν μητέρα μου καὶ τοὺς ἀδελφούς μου καὶ Σεμπρῶνιν καὶ τοὺς παρ᾽ αὐτοῦ.

(B.G.U. 385)

Serenilla sends warmest greetings to her father Socrates. Above all I hope that you are well and I say a prayer for you every day with the Lord Serapis and the other gods. I want you to know that I am lonely. Please remember that you have a daughter in Alexandria, so that I too may see that I have a father and people may see that I am not an orphan. To the bearer of this letter please give a reply about your health. I send greetings to my mother and my brothers and Sempronius and those with him.[10]

This letter also contains many errors of spelling, including ὑγιαίνιν for ὑγιαίνειν and ἱμί for εἰμί. One point of grammatical interest is that εἰς is used with the accusative case, as in ἰς Ἀλεξάνδρειαν to mean 'in Alexandria'. This is an example of the tendency to confuse motion towards with rest in something and is an early example of the move towards the elimination of the dative case. In modern Greek 'in Alexandria' would be εἰς τὴν Ἀλεξάνδρια or στὴν Ἀλεξάνδρια. In the same sentence ἔσσι is used instead of εἶ as the second person singular of εἰμί. In the κοινὴ διάλεκτος, unlike most –μι verbs which were transferred into verbs in –ω, εἰμί was conjugated as a middle voice:

	singular	plural
1	εἶμαι	εἴμεθα
2	εἶσαι	εἶσθε
3	ἔνι	ἔνι

In modern Greek the present tense of εἶμαι is as follows:

	singular	plural
1	εἶμαι	εἴμαστε
2	εἶσαι	εἶστε
3	εἶναι	εἶναι

The New Testament

We know very little about the writers of the New Testament for they did not date their books and they did not sign their names, except for Paul. Most of them would have had an Aramaic background but they wrote in the Greek κοινή. The Gospels, which were written during the first century AD, took their subject matter from what must have already been a strong oral tradition and the language they used would need to be readily intelligble to ordinary Christian worshippers or potential converts, not a literary or highly educated group. The style is simple but more formal than everyday speech would have been. There are as yet no marked changes in the basic forms and the changes in pronunciation are not apparent in the written texts. Co-ordinate clauses linked by such words as καί, γάρ, οὖν and τότε have largely taken the place of subordinate clauses and the Latin influence can be seen in such words as κῆνσος, Καῖσαρ and δηνάριος which have simply been transliterated into Greek.

St Luke II 8–11

Καὶ ποιμένες ἦσαν ἐν τῇ χώρᾳ τῇ αὐτῇ ἀγραυλοῦντες καὶ φυλάσσοντες φυλακὰς τῆς νυκτὸς ἐπὶ τὴν ποίμνην αὐτῶν. καὶ ἄγγελος Κυρίου ἐπέστη αὐτοῖς καὶ δόξα Κυρίου περιέλαμψεν αὐτούς, καὶ ἐφοβήθησαν φόβον μέγαν· καὶ εἶπεν αὐτοῖς ὁ ἄγγελος Μὴ φοβεῖσθε, ἰδοὺ γὰρ εὐαγγελίζομαι ὑμῖν χαρὰν μεγάλην ἥτις ἔσται παντὶ τῷ λαῷ, ὅτι ἐτέχθη ὑμῖν σήμερον σωτὴρ ὅς ἐστιν χριστὸς κύριος ἐν πόλει Δαυείδ·

Now in this same district there were shepherds out in the fields, keeping watch through the night over their flock, when suddenly there stood before them an angel of the Lord, and the splendour of the Lord shone around them. They were terror-struck but the angel said, 'Do not be afraid; I have good news for you: there is great joy coming to the whole people. Today in the city of David a deliverer has been born to you— the Messiah, the Lord.'[11]

Apart from its coordinated style with the frequent use of καὶ this passage also has examples of Semitic idiom. A verb is used with a cognate noun to give emphasis as in φυλάσσοντες φυλακὰς (keeping a close watch) and ἐφοβήθησαν φόβον μέγαν (they were greatly afraid).

St Matthew XXII 15–20

Τότε πορευθέντες οἱ Φαρισαῖοι συμβούλιον ἔλαβον ὅπως αὐτὸν παγιδεύσωσιν ἐν λόγῳ. καὶ ἀποστέλλουσιν αὐτῷ τοὺς μαθητὰς αὐτῶν μετὰ τῶν Ἡρῳδιανῶν λέγοντας Διδάσκαλε, οἴδαμεν ὅτι ἀληθὴς εἶ καὶ τὴν ὁδὸν τοῦ θεοῦ ἐν ἀληθείᾳ διδάσκεις, καὶ οὐ μέλει σοι περὶ οὐδενός, οὐ γὰρ βλέπεις εἰς πρόσωπον ἀνθρώπων· εἰπὸν οὖν ἡμῖν τί σοι δοκεῖ· ἔξεστιν δοῦναι κῆνσον Καίσαρι ἢ οὔ; γνοὺς δὲ ὁ Ἰησοῦς τὴν πονηρίαν αὐτῶν εἶπεν Τί με πειράζετε, ὑποκριταί; ἐπιδείξατέ μοι τὸ νόμισμα τοῦ κήνσου. οἱ δὲ προσήνεγκαν αὐτῷ δηνάριον. καὶ λέγει αὐτοῖς Τίνος ἡ εἰκὼν αὕτη καὶ ἡ ἐπιγραφή; λέγουσιν Καίσαρος. τότε λέγει αὐτοῖς Ἀπόδοτε οὖν τὰ Καίσαρος Καίσαρι καὶ τὰ τοῦ θεοῦ τῷ θεῷ. καὶ ἀκούσαντες ἐθαύμασαν, καὶ ἀφέντες αὐτὸν ἀπῆλθαν.

Then the Pharisees went and agreed on a plan to trap him in his own words. Some of their followers were sent to him in company with men of Herod's party. They said, 'Master, you are an honest man, we know; you teach in all honesty the way of life that God requires, truckling to no man, whoever he may be. Give us your ruling on this: are we or are we not permitted to pay taxes to the Roman Emperor?' Jesus was aware of their malicious intention and said to them, 'You hypocrites!

Why are you trying to catch me out? Show me the money in which the tax is paid'. They handed him a silver piece. Jesus asked, 'Whose head is this and whose inscription?' 'Caesar's', they replied. He said to them, 'Then pay to Caesar what is due to Caesar, and pay to God what is due to God'. This answer took them by surprise and they went away and left him alone.[12]

προσήνεγκαν, ἀπῆλθαν: the weak aorist ending (–αν) has replaced that of the strong aorist (–ον).
οἴδαμεν is a result of the regularisation of οἶδα.

	Ancient Greek		Κοινὴ Διάλεκτος	
	singular	plural	singular	plural
1	οἶδα	ἴσμεν	οἶδα	οἴδαμεν
2	οἶσθα	ἴστε	οἶδας	οἴδατε
3	οἶδε	ἴσασι(ν)	οἶδε	οἴδασι

Religious Poetry
The religious poetry of this period used a language which was a blend of Attic Greek and spoken forms. It consisted of metrically identical stanzas, often ending with the same refrain, which could be sung as hymns. The first letters of each stanza often formed an acrostic as in the Christmas Hymn of Romanos which has twenty-four stanzas giving the acrostic ΤΟΥ ΤΑΠΕΙΝΟΥ ΡΩΜΑΝΟΥ Ο ΥΜΝΟΣ. The extract included here is from an anonymous hymn thought to be of the sixth century AD and often attributed to Romanos. It is addressed to the Virgin Mary and is called the Akathistos (not seated) Hymn because it is sung before a standing congregation. It has twenty-four stanzas whose initial letters form the alphabet. After every other one the 'Alleluia' is sung, alternating with twelve 'Hails' which conclude χαῖρε, νύμφη ἀνύμφευτε (Hail, wedded maiden and virgin!)

In vocabulary and accidence the language of the hymn is good classical Greek. What marks it out as representative of its age is the simple style and syntax of the literary κοινή.

The Akathistos Hymn

Ἄγγελος πρωτοστάτης οὐρανόθεν ἐπέμφθη
    εἰπεῖν τῇ θεοτόκῳ τὸ ' χαῖρε '·
καὶ σὺν τῇ ἀσωμάτῳ φωνῇ

σωματούμενόν σε θεωρῶν,   κύριε,
ἐξίστατο καὶ ἵστατο,   κραυγάζων πρὸς αὐτὴν τοιαῦτα·
'χαῖρε, δι' ἧς ἡ χαρὰ ἐκλάμψει·
   χαῖρε, δι' ἧς ἡ ἀρὰ ἐκλείψει·
χαῖρε, τοῦ πεσόντος 'Αδὰμ ἡ ἀνάκλησις·
   χαῖρε, τῶν δακρύων τῆς Εὔας ἡ λύτρωσις·
χαῖρε, ὕψος δυσανάβατον   ἀνθρωπίνοις λογισμοῖς·
   χαῖρε, βάθος δυσθεώρητον   καὶ ἀγγέλων ὀφθαλμοῖς·
χαῖρε, ὅτι ὑπάρχεις   βασιλέως καθέδρα·
   χαῖρε, ὅτι βαστάζεις   τὸν βαστάζοντα πάντα·
χαῖρε, ἀστὴρ ἐμφαίνων τὸν ἥλιον·
   χαῖρε, γαστὴρ ἐνθέου σαρκώσεως·
χαῖρε, δι' ἧς νεουργεῖται ἡ κτίσις·
   χαῖρε, δι' ἧς βρεφουργεῖται ὁ κτίστης·
χαῖρε, νύμφη ἀνύμφευτε.'

Βλέπουσα ἡ ἁγία   ἑαυτὴν ἐν ἁγνείᾳ
   φησὶ τῷ Γαβριὴλ θαρσαλέως·
''τὸ παράδοξόν σου τῆς φωνῆς
   δυσπαράδεκτόν μου τῇ ψυχῇ   φαίνεται·
ἀσπόρου γὰρ συλλήψεως   τὴν κύησιν πῶς λέγεις κράζων·
            'Αλληλούϊα; ''

Γνῶσιν ἄγνωστον γνῶναι   ἡ παρθένος ζητοῦσα
   ἐβόησε πρὸς τὸν λειτουργοῦντα·
''ἐκ λαγόνων ἁγνῶν υἱὸν
   πῶς ἐστι τεχθῆναι δυνατόν; λέξον μοι. ''
Πρὸς ἣν ἐκεῖνος ἔφησεν ἐν φόβῳ,   πλὴν κραυγάζων
                  οὕτω·
''χαῖρε, βουλῆς ἀπορρήτου μύστις,
   χαῖρε, σιγῆς δεομένων πίστις·
χαῖρε, τῶν θαυμάτων Χριστοῦ τὸ προοίμιον,
   χαῖρε, τῶν δογμάτων αὐτοῦ τὸ κεφάλαιον·
χαῖρε, κλῖμαξ ἐπουράνιε,   ᾗ κατέβη ὁ θεός,
   χαῖρε, γέφυρα μετάγουσα   τοὺς ἐκ γῆς πρὸς οὐρανόν·
χαῖρε, τὸ τῶν ἀγγέλων   πολυθρύλητον θαῦμα·
   χαῖρε, τὸ τῶν δαιμόνων   πολυθρήνητον τραῦμα·
χαῖρε, τὸ φῶς ἀρρήτως γεννήσασα·
   χαῖρε, τὸ ''πῶς'' μηδένα διδάξασα·
χαῖρε, σοφῶν ὑπερβαίνουσα γνῶσιν·

27

χαῖρε, πιστῶν καταυγάζουσα φρένας·
χαῖρε, νύμφη ἀνύμφευτε. "

The leading angel was sent from heaven to say to the Virgin: 'Hail'.
And when he saw you, O Lord, becoming flesh, he was amazed and
arose and cried to her with voice incorporeal:
    'Hail to you through whom joy will shine out;
    hail to you through whom the curse shall pass away;
    hail, redemption of fallen Adam;
    hail, deliverance of the tears of Eve;
    hail, height unattainable by human thought;
    hail, depth invisible even to the eyes of angels;
    hail to you, the throne of the king;
    hail to you who bear him, the bearer of all;
    hail, star that heralds the sun;
    hail, womb of divine incarnation;
    hail to you through whom creation is reborn;
    hail to you through whom the Creator becomes a child;
    hail, wedded maiden and virgin.'
The holy lady, seeing herself to be chaste, spoke boldly to Gabriel:
'The paradox of your words I find hard for my soul to accept; what do
you mean when you speak of childbirth from a conception without
seed, crying 'Alleluia'?'
    The Virgin, yearning to grasp a knowledge unknowable, cried to the
ministering angel: 'How can a son be born of chaste loins, tell me?'
    He himself spoke to her in fear; yet this he cried:
    'Hail, initiate of secret counsel;
    hail to you, the proof of knowledge that demands silence;
    hail, prelude to the miracles of Christ;
    hail, the sum of his teachings;
    hail, celestial ladder by which God has descended;
    hail, bridge that bears men from earth to heaven;
    hail, far-famed miracle of the angels;
    hail, much-mourned affliction of the spirits of evil;
    hail to you, mysterious mother of light;
    hail to you, who taught nobody 'how';
    hail to you, surpassing the knowledge of the wise;
    hail to you, illuminating the minds of the faithful;
    hail, wedded maiden and virgin.'[13]

The years between 600 and 1100 saw many movements and changes in ways of life within the Byzantine Empire but we have very little evidence for how the Greek language itself was affected. A policy of centralisation discouraged developments outside Constantinople and inside the city a devotion to the classical heritage meant that most learned men advocated the use of a reconstructed form of the pure Attic dialect. Therefore, although it has been established that by 1000 AD the spoken language had assumed most of the characteristics of modern Greek and that the major changes had already occurred in the period up to the sixth century AD, the majority of the literature of the time is of no help in tracing the stages of the development of spoken Greek during this period.

There is a vast body of religious literature in the purist style and, on the secular side, there are histories, rhetoric, philosophy, philology and grammar. We should not forget that we owe much to the Byzantines for the preservation of the literature of ancient Greece.

Amongst literature of the period which is less polished and, therefore, of more relevance to a study of the spoken language, can be included certain chronicles and collections of stories. Chronicles were written by priests or monks, for example, to provide illustrations of the Christian faith to their readers. John Malalas (491–578) wrote a narrative from the Creation to his own day and a later chronicle of 'Monk George' had a similar span. **John Moschus** (550–619) put together a collection of stories about monks, known as the *Spiritual Meadow*, which, although influenced by the literary and church tradition, would be easily intelligible to ordinary people as was the New Testament.

In one of his tales, a notorious brigand suddenly decides to mend his ways. He begs to enter a monastery and, once admitted, he proves to be outstanding for his self-control, piety and humility. One day an angel appears to him and tells him that the Lord has forgiven all his sins. When the former brigand, David, expresses his doubts as to whether God could forgive him in such a short time, the angel punishes his lack of faith by binding his tongue and removing from him the power of speech. The short extract given below starts with David's reply.

> '"Όταν ἤμην εἰς τὸν κόσμον τὰ ἀθέμιτα καὶ τὰς αἱματοχυσίας ποιῶν ἐλάλουν, καὶ ὅτε θέλω δουλεῦσαι τῷ Θεῷ καὶ ὕμνους αὐτῷ προσφέρειν τὴν γλῶσσάν μου δεσμεύεις τοῦ μὴ λαλεῖν;"

Τότε ὁ ἄγγελος ἀπεκρίθη λέγων· "Ἔση εἰς τὸν κανόνα μόνον λαλῶν, ἔξωθεν δὲ τοῦ κανόνος σιωπῶν τὸ παράπαν." Ὅπερ καὶ γέγονεν. Πολλὰ γὰρ σημεῖα δι' αὐτοῦ ὁ Θεὸς ἐποίησεν. Ἔψαλλεν δὲ τοὺς ψαλμοὺς, ἄλλο δὲ ῥῆμα ἢ μέγα ἢ μικρὸν οὐκ ἠδύνατο λαλῆσαι.

Ἰωάννου Μόσχου   Λειμῶν Πνευματικός 143

'When I was in the world, committing acts of lawlessness and shedding blood, I talked all the time and (now) when I want to serve the Lord and offer hymns to Him, are you binding my tongue and preventing me from talking?'

Then the angel replied to him, saying 'You will only talk in the Canon; outside the Canon you will be completely silent.'

And this was so. For God gave many signs through him. He chanted the psalms but was unable to utter any other word, big or small.

This extract shows the infinitive still in use as in θέλω δουλεῦσαι...καὶ προσφέρειν and οὐκ ἠδύνατο λαλῆσαι. It is used after the article in the genitive case in τὴν γλῶσσαν μου δεσμεύεις τοῦ μὴ λαλεῖν. The present active participle also survives, ποιῶν and λέγων, and its use in Ἔση...λαλῶν...σιωπῶν gives us an example of the substitution of a periphrastic expression for the classical future tense.

The now familiar use of εἰς + accusative in the sense of 'rest in a place' is seen in εἰς τὸν κόσμον.

ἤμην (imperfect) for classical ἦ or ἦν is an example of the development in the verb 'to be' which occurred during this period. The change in the present tense of the verb 'to be' from irregular endings to a more regular medio-passive form was discussed earlier (page 24). The new medio-passive forms of the imperfect tense are as follows:

	singular	plural
1	ἤμην	ἤμεθα
2	ἦσο	ἦσασθε
3	ἦτο(ν)	ἦσαν, ἦν, ἦταν

In modern Greek the corresponding conjugation is:

	singular	plural
1	ἤμουν(α)	ἤμαστε
2	ἤσουν(α)	ἤσαστε
3	ἦταν, ἤτανε	ἦταν, ἤτανε, ἦσαν

30

Of course, the survival of an old form and the occurrence of a new form are not mutually exclusive. Writers would be influenced by both the spoken language and the literary tradition. We can only notice signs of change and development; no categorical statement can be made about the exact form of the language at any particular point in time.

Some of the works of the **Emperor Constantine VII Porphyrogenitus** (908–959) are also useful for the study of the spoken language. He was only a child when he became Emperor and for much of his life he let others take charge of the government of the Empire while he devoted himself to research and writings. His manuals on administration and imperial ceremonial cannot be called great literature but they have proved to be valuable sources of detail for later historians. Their value for the study of the Greek language lies in the fact that they are practical rather than theoretical writings and include much new technical vocabulary. Constantine Porphyrogenitus states in his introduction that it is his intention to use the common language of the people. At the beginning of the *De Administrando Imperio*, and using Attic Greek, he gives the following advice to his son:

Οὐ γὰρ ἐπίδειξιν καλλιγραφίας ἢ φράσεως ἠττικισμένης καὶ τὸ διηρμένον διογκούσης καὶ ὑψηλὸν ποιῆσαι ἐσπούδασα, ἀλλὰ μᾶλλον διὰ κοινῆς καὶ καθωμιλημένης ἀπαγγελίας διδάξαι σοι ἔσπευσα, ἅπερ οἴομαι δεῖν σε μὴ ἀγνοεῖν...

For I have not been studious to make a display of fine writing or of an Atticising style, swollen with the sublime and lofty, but rather have been eager by means of everyday and conversational narrative to teach you those things of which I think you should not be ignorant.[14]

His prefaces are all in Attic Greek but in the rest of his work the language is mixed. Arnold Toynbee writes that 'neither Constantine nor any other Byzantine writer in Greek ever wrote the actual language that he spoke— not even when his literary guards were down', but he adds in a footnote that he did, at least twice, so far forget himself as to write νερό.[15]

The following extract is part of a detailed description from his register of the Byzantine court etiquette, *De Caerimoniis*. This particular passage, which describes the Emperor preparing to go to the Hippodrome, shows many Latin words adapted into Greek and a very simple syntax, mostly consisting of co-ordinate clauses linked by καὶ and δὲ.

31

ὁ δὲ βασιλεὺς περιβαλλόμενος τὸ χρυσοπερίκλειστον αὐτοῦ σαγίον καὶ δηριγευόμενος ὑπὸ τῶν ἀρχόντων τοῦ κουβουκλείου, διέρχεται διὰ τῶν διαβατικῶν τοῦ Τρικόγχου, ᾿Αψίδος τε καὶ τῆς Δάφνης, ἅπτων κηροὺς ἐν τοῖς εὐκτηρίοις, ὡς εἴθισται αὐτῷ...

...

...εἰσέρχεται δὲ ὁ βασιλεὺς ἐν τῷ κοιτῶνι αὐτοῦ, καὶ προσκαλεσάμενος ὁ πραιπόσιτος τοὺς βεστήτορας, εἰσέρχον-ται καὶ περιβάλλουσιν τὴν χλανίδα τῷ βασιλεῖ, εἰπόντος δὲ τοῦ πραιποσίτου· ᾿Κελεύσατε᾿ ἐξέρχονται οἱ βεστήτορες ἀπὸ τοῦ κοιτῶνος, καὶ στεφθεὶς ὑπὸ τοῦ πραιποσίτου ὁ βασιλεὺς ἐξέρχεται ἀπὸ τοῦ κοιτῶνος, δηριγευόμενος ὑπὸ τῶν ἀρχόντων τοῦ κουβουκλείου. στὰς δὲ εἰς τὸ στενόν, νεύει τῷ πραιποσίτῳ, ὁ δὲ πραιπόσιτος τῷ ὀστιαρίῳ, καὶ ὁ ὀστιάριος εἰσάγει τοὺς πατρικίους, τὸ δὲ βῆλον τῆς πύλης ἐκείνης σιλεντιάριος ποιεῖ.

Εἰσελθόντες δὲ ἔσω οἱ πατρίκιοι μετὰ καὶ τῶν στρατηγῶν, πίπτουσιν, καὶ ἀναστάντων αὐτῶν, νεύει ὁ βασιλεὺς τῷ πραιποσίτῳ, καὶ λέγει μεγάλως· ᾿Κελεύσατε᾿...

...Δηριγευόμενος δὲ, ὡς προείρηται, ὑπ᾿ αὐτῶν πάντων ὁ βασιλεὺς ἐξέρχεται καὶ ἀνέρχεται ἐν τῷ καθίσματι, καὶ στὰς ἔμπροσθεν τοῦ σένζου, σφραγίζει τὸν λαὸν ἐκ γ᾿, πρῶτον μὲν μέσον, δεύτερον τὸν τοῦ Βενέτου δῆμον, τρίτον τοῦ Πρασίνου, καὶ καθέζεται ἐπὶ τοῦ σένζου.[16]

(῎Εκθεσις βασιλείου τάξεως σ. 304a–307)

The Emperor, putting on his gold-edged cloak and escorted by his chamberlains, passes through the corridors of the Triconchos, the Apse and the Daphne, lighting candles in the oratories as was his custom...
...The Emperor enters his bedchamber and his dressers, summoned by the Lord Chamberlain, come in and help the Emperor to put on his coat. Then, when the Lord Chamberlain says 'Please!', the dressers leave the bedchamber and the Emperor, after being crowned by the Lord Chamberlain, comes out of his room escorted by the gentlemen of the bedchamber. Standing in the narrow corridor, he makes a sign to the Lord Chamberlain who makes a sign to the doorman. The doorman leads in the patricians while a silentiary gives the signal for the beginning of the races. The patricians, having entered with the generals, fall to their knees and, after they have risen, the Emperor makes another sign to the Lord Chamberlain and says in a loud voice, 'Please!'...

Escorted, as has been described earlier, by all these people, the Emperor comes out and mounts his special seat. Standing in front of the throne he makes the sign of the cross over the people three times, first in the centre, then over the faction of the Blues and finally over the faction of the Greens. He then takes his seat on the throne.

Classical words with new meanings include the following:
ὁ βασιλεύς: the Greek word for 'king' has supplanted the Latin word 'imperator' as the official title for an Eastern Roman Emperor.
κελεύσατε: when used as a word of ceremony, this corresponds to 'please' or 'be pleased'.
σφραγίζω (to seal): this has the additional meaning of 'to make the sign of the cross'.
ὁ δῆμος (deme): this has acquired an additional specialised meaning. It came to refer to the faction of supporters for a particular team of chari-oteers at the race-course (the Hippodrome). These factions, the Blues and the Greens, later developed into specific political and social groups.

Words derived from Latin are:
διριγεύω < dirigo dirigere—to direct, lead
τὸ κουβούκλειον < cubiculum—bedroom
ὁ πραιπόσιτος < praepositus—one put in charge, the chief of the emperor's eunuchs
οἱ βεστήτορες < vestitores—dressers
ὁ ὁστιάριος < ostiarius—doorman
οἱ πατρίκιοι < patricii—patricians, nobles
τὸ βῆλον < velum—sail, awning, curtain; the signal for beginning the races at the Hippodrome
ὁ σιλεντιάριος < silentiarius—one who calls for silence
ὁ σέντζος < sessus—the emperor's throne

The beginning of the elimination of the dative case can be seen where the locative ἐν + dative is generally replaced by εἰς + accusative e.g. στὰς δὲ εἰς τὸ στενόν (lines 9–10). At the same time, there is still some confusion, as can be illustrated by the following examples in which ἐν + dative has been used for 'motion towards':
εἰσέρχεται ὁ βασιλεὺς ἐν τῷ κοιτῶνι (line 6)
ἀνέρχεται ἐν τῷ καθίσματι (line 22).

As has been seen, evidence for the spoken language is scanty for the early

33

Middle Ages and much of the evaluation of the language made by scholars has had to be retrospective. The gulf between the official language and the spoken language was wide, a situation which was to become a problem again during the early years of Greek independence in the nineteenth century. This was still a dilemma at the beginning of the twentieth century and, in fact, it is only since the 1970s that there has been effective action to bring together into one standard form both Katharevousa, the purist style, and Demotic, the language of everyday conversation.

Written literature in the popular idiom is not found until the twelfth century AD when the Empire had already begun to fall into the hands of invaders and the old centralisation was lost. From the thirteenth century onwards we begin to find literature being written in the spoken idiom in a variety of localities. In areas under foreign rule this was one of the ways in which the Greek language was so well preserved.

CHAPTER THREE

GREECE UNDER FRANKISH AND TURKISH DOMINATION:
THIRTEENTH—EIGHTEENTH CENTURY AD

In April 1204 AD the Frankish crusaders, aided or rather led by the Venetians, captured Constantinople. The ultimate goal of this Fourth Crusade was the conquest of Egypt and the liberation of the Holy Land but the Doge of Venice, Enrico Dandolo, had other ideas. When the Franks could not pay their dues to him, he persuaded them to divert their voyage. They sacked Zara in Dalmatia and then proceeded to the Great City itself. The reasons for the assault on Constantinople are complex, compounded of political intrigue to restore the deposed Emperor Isaac II Angelus or his son, desire for revenge for anti-Venetian riots in the City, religious differences and the commercial ambitions of the Venetians. This was only the last of a series of setbacks suffered by the Byzantine Empire at the end of the twelfth century but the resulting sack of a Christian city by a Christian army was a ghastly crime. The scale of massacre and looting was appalling; priceless treasures were destroyed or removed and great works of literature were lost.

Count Baldwin of Flanders was elected Emperor to rule over a restricted Latin Empire around Constantinople, while the rest of the former Byzantine territory was divided up between the Franks and the Venetians. This meant that until the coming of the Turks in the fifteenth century, the Greek world was split up into many different feudal states. The Franks were assigned lands on the mainland of Greece and the Venetians took control of many of the coastal areas and most of the islands, including Crete. The Latin Empire only lasted until 1261 AD when there was a limited revival of the former Byzantine Empire in the area around Constantinople, but some of the Frankish and Venetian states continued their existence for two or three hundred years. Crete remained a Venetian possession until the seventeenth century, and the Peloponnese was ruled by the Franks for several generations. The essential character of the

35

Greek nation, however, was not greatly affected. The Franks failed to convert the Greeks to Roman Catholicism and it was they themselves who changed their language, adopting that of the conquered Greeks amongst whom they lived.

We are given a good picture of the feudal type of society which was established during the Frankish occupation in a history in verse called the *Chronicle of the Morea*. This was written by a Greek-speaking Frank in the fourteenth century and is an account of the establishment of Frankish control in the Peloponnese.

Meanwhile, on the eastern borders of the Byzantine Empire, there had been composed an epic poem whose hero, Digenis Akritis, was the son of an Arab father and a Greek mother. He was known as Digenis because he was born of two races and Akritis because he lived on and defended the frontiers between the Byzantine and Arab Empires. The poem was probably originally composed in the eleventh century, although it has its historical setting in the eighth or ninth century. It was inspired by the deeds of the border fighters in the district of the Tigris and the Euphrates, but at the time when the poem was written there must have been peace on the frontier, for its theme is one of co-operation between Christians and Arabs. The original poem was composed in a literary style of Greek but the name Digenis is also found in a great cycle of folk songs composed in the language of the people. In this later Akritic cycle of ballads Digenis is only one of a number of heroes and there is very little connection with the original epic. The name he is given in the folk songs is Akritas but it never has the significance of 'frontiersman' and no use is made of the idea of double birth implied in the name Digenis. These later ballads are best considered as part of the large collection of Greek folk songs whose origins are obscure but whose popularity was widespread and whose value for our study lies in the closeness of their language to everyday speech. The heroic exploits and supernatural elements in the Akritic ballads also had considerable influence on subsequent Greek literature.

The Byzantine Empire finally came to an end in May 1453 when the Turkish Sultan Mohammed II captured Constantinople. Less than ten years later the Turks had gained control of most of the Greek mainland, although Crete, Cyprus and Rhodes remained under Western rule for some time, and the Ionian islands never passed to the Turks.

The history of the next few centuries, however, is not one of a downtrodden and oppressed nation, as is sometimes popularly supposed. Constantinople remained a centre of Greek leadership under the Patriarch who was appointed by the Sultan as Ethnarch, the leader of all the conquered Orthodox Christians. There was also much literary and intellectual activity, particularly in Crete, Cyprus, the Ionian islands and Italy. Those interested in the Cypriot literature of the period should read Τὸ Χρονικὸ Τοῦ Μαχαιρά (fifteenth century) and the sixteenth century Cypriot *Love Songs*. The importance of Italy extended beyond the direct influence of Venetian rule. Many learned Greeks left their homelands to go to Italy, where they made a major contribution to the Renaissance. Classical study was admired there and there was a certain prestige in being a Hellene. At the University of Padua the courses in philosophy and medicine were particularly popular and the study of Greek was generally encouraged. Venice was a lively centre of Greek culture by the end of the fifteenth century AD with libraries of Greek manuscripts and with printing presses for the publication of texts. Later a few national schools were refounded in Greece with an emphasis on classical studies, philosophy and science.

After 1453 the cultural life of Crete was enriched by the arrival of refugees from Constantinople. At the same time the influence of the Franks and Venetians provided models for the development of drama and verse romances. By the beginning of the seventeenth century Crete was famous for both. Its drama consisted of tragedies and some comedies. The two main writers associated with the Cretan drama of the seventeenth century are Georgios Chortatzis and Vitsentzos Kornaros. Chortatzis is thought to have been the author of a grim tragedy *Erophile* and Kornaros of a beautiful religious play, the *Sacrifice of Abraham*, an original interpretation of an Italian model, full of fine character drawing and human warmth.

The romances of the West were tales of brave and chivalrous heroes whose exploits, performed for love and highly exaggerated, were described in verse. Greek adaptations of these, influenced also by Hellenistic verse romances, were current before the fall of Constantinople, although we do not know anything about the writers. *Callimachos and Chrysorrhoe* and *Lybistros and Rhodamne* are examples of these. Conditions in Crete in the seventeenth century, with Byzantine, Venetian and Frankish influence, were ideal for the development of this type of poetry and the culmination was the *Erotocritos*, generally considered to be the masterpiece of Cretan literature. This was written by Vitsentzos Kornaros not long before the Turks captured Crete in 1669. He modelled it on a French romance, *Paris et Vienne*, which he found in an Italian version, but the story is set in Athens and its spirit is Greek. This mixture of influences is typical of the period when Greece was under Western rule.

Although the poem was European in origin, its language was the spoken idiom of Crete and it was quickly established there as a folk song.

After the fall of Crete, Greek refugees arrived in the Ionian islands and then it was the turn of that area of the Greek world to continue the Greek literary tradition. A good example of how a work might survive and travel during these centuries can be seen in the first edition of the *Erotocritos*. This was printed in Venice in 1713 and, in the introduction, the editor wrote that it was 'an old poem...which is...praised and honoured in the islands of the Adriatic, and in the Peloponnese, and indeed in the famous land of Zakynthos, where are still to be found the descendants of the wretched Cretans who found a friendly refuge there after the capture of their country. It was these who popularised the poem, which is composed in the natural Cretan tongue, and spread it throughout the island, and to other places, where it appears most pleasant and graceful to all such as read it'.[17]

In Greece itself, the Turks in no way tried to stamp out Greek culture. Although the Greeks lost much freedom of action, they did not lose their identity. The Turks administered their empire without forcing their own customs, religion or language on the conquered nations. Mohammed II, the conqueror of Constantinople, had admired the Greeks and he also realised that he could rule best with their co-operation. He allowed freedom of worship to the Orthodox Christians and, as a guarantee, he gave responsibility for the behaviour of the Greeks to the Patriarch of Constantinople who was the religious head of the nation. He even increased the Greek population of Constantinople by bringing in wealthy citizens from Trebizond and a few other areas. As a result of this encouragement, there emerged a number of influential merchant families within the Greek community. They were known as Phanariots because they lived in the Phanar quarter of the city, near the Patriarchate. The Phanariots admired learning and they played a major role in keeping alive Greek culture. It was the Phanariots who were employed to conduct the foreign relations of the Ottoman empire and were chosen to be rulers of the Danubian principalities of Wallachia and Moldavia which were subject to the Turks. There they founded Greek universities at Bucharest and Jassy.

A wealthy Greek, therefore, would have had little trouble in getting a good education, if he could afford to travel or if he lived in a big city. In the provinces the majority of the population had little literary education, a situation no different from that in many other European countries at the time, but they did have schools run by the clergy. It was only in cases of local persecution that schools were closed and this was the exception rather than the rule. The teaching in these schools would have been religious and moral but, unfortunately, there was no link between these schools and the higher academies with their philosophical and rationalist curricula.

It is not so much in the centres of learning, however, as amongst the people that developments in the language can be traced. Turning away, therefore, from the cities, we find a large body of ballad poetry in the provinces. This must have been sung in the villages for many generations before it was finally recorded and published in the nineteenth century. In the eighteenth century, European travellers in Greece commented on the existence of folk songs which were composed in the oral manner and were very popular. Τά δημοτικά τραγούδια reflect the lives of the mainland Greeks. They include songs of everyday life, such as lullabies, wedding songs and dirges, as well as folk tales and historical songs. Some of the most famous are known as the Klephtic ballads.

As the centuries of Turkish rule passed, bandits, known as Klephts, had gone up into the mountains, making their living by raiding and plundering. The Turkish authorities countered this type of rebellion by bribing one group of Greeks to hold off the other. The group to whom the Turks designated this policing role were called the Armatoli (men at arms) but they had eventually become disgruntled with their masters and by the end of the eighteenth century, they too had joined the Klephts. Thus C.M. Woodhouse writes: 'The fineness of the distinction [between Klephts and Armatoli], as well as the chronic anarchy natural to the mountains, cannot be better summarised than in the line of a popular song, in which a dying brigand-leader describes himself as "thirty years an Armatolos and twenty years a Klepht." '[18] This anarchy was primarily a social phenomenon but, in the poems, both groups are glamorised as defenders of freedom against the Turks.

All of this Greek ballad poetry has no obvious outside influences and no historical influences beyond the preceding generations during which the poems were handed down. It can, therefore, give us a good picture of the natural and living language of the people.

As a brief illustration of the literature of the period from the thirteenth to the eighteenth centuries, extracts are given from the *Chronicle of the Morea*, the *Sacrifice of Abraham*, the *Erotocritos* and the ballad poetry of the mainland, all of which reflect the spoken Greek language of their time and place. In the language of this period there is new vocabulary from French, Italian and Turkish sources and there are some developments in grammar. What is significant for us is that it is only now that the major changes of the previous centuries become apparent.

Τὸ Χρονικὸν Τοῦ Μορέως (*The Chronicle of the Morea*) Fourteenth century AD.
There are several versions of the *Chronicle of the Morea*, written in Greek, French, Aragonese and Italian. The Greek version is the only one that is in verse. It is thought to have been composed at about 1388 and to have been an expanded translation of a French original. Even after one generation the Franks of the Peloponnese had assimilated Greek ways so far as to be bilingual; by the middle of the fourteenth century, after over one hundred years of occupation, Greek was the natural language of the resident Franks for whom this version of the Chronicle was composed. The poem is Greek in language only. Its spirit, with its ideals of knightly excellence, is thoroughly foreign. The poet was a Catholic Frank who attacked the Greeks for their cowardice and deceitfulness while depicting the Franks as brave and virtuous. He wrote in verse so that his work could be listened to in recitation as well as be read.

The language of the poem is a form of medieval Greek which is open to much criticism but, because it was written without any scholastic pretensions, it represents the poet's own natural idiom and gives us an example of a style of Greek which was acceptable in its own time and place. From the point of view of the development of the language, it reveals many of the simplifications of grammar and adaptations of vocabulary which are typical of medieval and modern Greek. It is the first use of the spoken Greek language for recording history.

In the extract which follows we are told how William of Champlitte decided to sail to Greece to claim a kingdom there. The story of Champlitte given by the writer of the poem is not valid historically, for Champlitte had, in fact, gone to the East with the Fourth Crusade and it was on his return from there that he had entered the Peloponnese in the army of Boniface, the king of Salonica. While he was engaged in the siege of Nauplion he had been joined by an old friend, Geoffrey de Villehardouin, and together they had set out on an expedition of conquest in the Peloponnese which resulted in them gaining control of almost the whole peninsula. They created twelve major fiefs which were subdivided and distributed among the Frankish nobles. The later history of Champlitte records how he eventually returned to France, perhaps to claim the inheritance from his brother Louis who had died there. He died himself before he could return to Greece. Geoffrey de Villehardouin was eventually to emerge as the Lord of the Morea.

40

Κι ὡσὰν ἀκούσουν κ' ἔμαθαν τὸ πῶς οἱ Φράγκοι ἐκεῖνοι,
ὅπου ὑπαγαῖναν στὴν Συρίαν μὲ θέλημα τοῦ Πάπα,
ἀφῆκαν τὸ ταξεῖδιν τους κι ἀπῆλθαν εἰς τὴν Πόλιν
κ' ἐκέρδισαν τὴν Ρωμανίαν κ' ἐγίνησαν ἀφέντες,
βουλὴν ἀπήρασιν ὁμοῦ ἐκεῖνοι οἱ δύο αὐταδέλφοι·
νὰ μείνῃ ἕνας ἀπὸ αὐτοὺς ἐκεῖ εἰς τὸ ἰγονικόν τους,
κι ὁ ἄλλος νὰ ἀπέλθη εἰς Ρωμανίαν διὰ νὰ κερδίσῃ
                                                          τόπον.
Λοιπὸν ὡς τὸ ἔχει ἐριζικὸν ἡ χάρις τῶν ἀνθρώπων,
κι οὐδὲν ὁμοιάζουν οἱ ἀδελφοὶ εἰς πρόσοψιν καὶ χάριν,
ἦτον ὁ ὑστερνότερος ἀπὸ τοὺς δύο αὐταδέλφους,
ὁκάτι ἐπιδεξιώτερος καὶ φρονιμώτερός τους.
Κ' ἰσιάστησαν οἱ δύο ἀδελφοί, ὁ πρῶτος ν' ἐνεμείνῃ
ἐκεῖσε εἰς τὸ κοντᾶτο του ἐκεῖνο τῆς Τσαμπάνιας,
κι ὁ δεύτερος ἀπὸ τοὺς δύο μισὶρ Γουλιάμος ἄκω,
εἶχεν καὶ ἐπίκλην ὁ λόγου του, τὸν ἐλέγαν ντὲ Σαλοῦθε
νὰ εὕρη φουσσᾶτα ὅσα ἠμπορεῖ νὰ ἐπάρῃ μετὰ ἐκεῖνον,
κ' ἐκεῖνος νὰ ἔλθη εἰς Ρωμανίαν τοῦ νὰ ἔχῃ κουγκεστήσει
κάστρη καὶ χώρας τίποτε νὰ τὰ ἔχῃ ἰγονικά του.
Ὁ κόντος γὰρ τοῦ ἐξέδωκεν ὅσον λογάριν εἶχε,
καὶ εἶπεν του· «Ἀδελφούτσικε, ἀφῶν ἐγὼ ἐνεμένω
ἀφέντης εἰς τὰ κάστρη μας κ' εἰς τὸ ἰγονικόν μας,
ἔπαρε τὸ λογάριν μας καὶ τὰ κοινά μας ὅλα
κι ἄμε μὲ τὴν εὐχίτσα μου ὁμοίως καὶ τοῦ πατρός μας,
κ' ἐλπίζω εἰς τὸ ἔλεος τοῦ Θεοῦ ὅτι νὰ εὐτυχήσῃς».

lines 1366–89

And when they heard the news that those Franks, who had been on their way to Syria by the will of the Pope, had abandoned their journey, gone off to the city, won 'Romania' and become masters, then those two brothers together adopted a plan for one of them to remain there in their family estate and for the other to go to 'Romania' to win a place there.

But, as human happiness always has in it an element of fate, and since the two brothers were in no way alike in looks or character, the younger of the two was somewhat more skilled and wiser. Thus the two brothers made an agreement that the elder should stay there in that county of his in Champagne and that the younger, called Sir William, but also having a surname of his own by which he was known as 'de Salute', was to find as large a contingent as he could to take with him.

He was to go to 'Romania' and, having won some castles and lands, to have them as his portion. For the count gave him all the cash he had and said to him:

'Dear brother, since I am staying behind as master in our castles and family estate, take our ready cash and all our assets and go with the blessing of both myself and our father. And I hope, by the mercy of God, that you will have good fortune.'

N.B. Ρωμανία: After the fall of the Western Roman Empire this word continued to be used to describe the Greek-speaking Eastern Empire. The words Ρωμαῖοι or Ρωμιοί are frequently found in use as the equivalent of Ἕλληνες, as in the demotic song of 1821 about the Greek hero Athanasius Diakos. When asked whether he would be willing to become a Turk and change his religion in order to save his life, he answered: ' Ρωμιὸς ἐγὼ γεννήθηκα, Ρωμιὸς θενὰ πεθάνω' (I was born a Greek and I shall die a Greek).

Grammatical points

i) The simplification of first declension masculine nouns is illustrated by the retention of the vowel –α in the genitive singular of τοῦ Πάπα and the substitution of –ες for –αι in ἀφέντες.

ii) A regular feature of the Greek of this period is the loss of the final –ν in the accusative singular, as in τὴν εὐχίτσα.

The modern Greek categorisation of declensions uses a simple symmetrical system in which there are two main groups of nouns, one comprising nouns which have two different endings and the other those which have three endings. These two groups are referred to as δικατάληκτα/δίπτωτα and τρικατάληκτα/ τρίπτωτα.

e.g. **Nouns with two endings**

sing.	nom.	πατέρας	ἐργάτης	χώρα	φωνή
	acc.	πατέρα	ἐργάτη	χώρα	φωνή
	gen.	πατέρα	ἐργάτη	χώρας	φωνῆς
pl.	nom.	πατέρες	ἐργάτες	χῶρες	φωνές
	acc.	πατέρες	ἐργάτες	χῶρες	φωνές
	gen.	πατέρων	ἐργάτων	χώρων	φωνῶν

Nouns with three endings

sing.	nom.	λόγος
	acc.	λόγο

	gen.	λόγου
pl.	nom.	λόγοι
	acc.	λόγους
	gen.	λόγων

Added to these patterns are neuter nouns, which are all of two endings, such as δέντρο gen. δέντρου, παιδί gen. παιδιοῦ, ὄνομα gen. ὀνόματος and λάθος gen. λάθους.

The simplification of the ancient Greek third declension pattern of σκέψις σκέψεως to a two-ending noun is described later, on page 52.

iii) τὸ ταξεῖδιν and τὸ λογάριν are examples of the simplification of nouns ending in -ιον e.g. τὸ ταξείδιον > τὸ ταξεῖδιν, and when the final -ν is also lost the Modern Greek word τὸ ταξεῖδι, ταξίδι (a journey) remains.

The same tendency can be seen in the modern forms of proper names ending in -ιος. 'Αντώνης is derived from Αντώνιος as follows:

'Αντώνιος acc. 'Αντώνιον > 'Αντῶνιν > 'Αντῶνι ('Αντώνη).

Then from the new accusative 'Αντώνη there is formed a new nominative 'Αντώνης.

In the same way Δημήτριος becomes Δημήτρης.

iv) The simplification of the past tense of the verb can be seen in the following examples:

ἔμαθαν, ἀπῆλθαν—elimination of the strong aorist ending –ον
ὑπαγαῖναν—imperfect ending in –αν

v) The following prepositional phrases illustrate the loss of the dative and the tendency towards the use of the accusative case after prepositions:

εἰς τὰ κάστρη—in the castles
εἰς τὸ ἰγονικόν τους—in their inheritance
εἰς τὸ κοντᾶτο—in the county
(ἐν + dative → εἰς + accusative)
μετὰ ἐκεῖνον—with him (genitive → accusative)
μὲ τὴν εὐχίτσα—with the prayer (genitive → accusative)
(N.B. μὲ is the modern Greek equivalent of μετά in its sense of 'with')
ἀπὸ αὐτούς—from them (genitive → accusative)

vi) The genitive is used instead of the dative for the indirect object:

τοῦ εξέδωκεν, εἶπεν του

vii) The use of τοῦ for αὐτοῦ in the above examples is paralleled by the following:

τὸ κοντᾶτο του—his county

τὸν ἔλεγαν—they called him
τὸ ταζεῖδιν τους—their journey
ὁ...φρονιμώτερός τους—the wiser of them
The development of these third person pronouns is from αὐτόν αὐτήν
etc. and has nothing to do with the definite article. Note that the enclitic
form of the accusative plural is also used for the genitive plural. The same
tendency is seen in the plural of the first and second person pronouns.

e.g. τὸ λογάριν μας, τοῦ πατρός μας
viii) νὰ is an abbreviated form of the ancient Greek ἵνα and is used with
the subjunctive not only to express purpose but also as an alternative to
most uses of the infinitive.

e.g. διὰ νὰ κερδίσῃ—in order to win
βουλὴν ἀπήρασιν...νὰ μείνῃ—they adopted a plan (for one of
them) to stay
ἰσιάστησαν...ὁ πρῶτος ν'ἐνεμείνῃ...κι ὁ δεύτερος...νὰ εὕρῃ
—they made an agreement that the elder should stay there...and that
the younger one should find...

Vocabulary
i) Words derived from Latin:
φουσσᾶτον = fossatum—fortified place, camp, but here used in the
sense of 'armed force'
κάστρη = castra—fort, castle
ii) Adaptations of ancient Greek words:
ταξείδι(ο)ν—diminutive of τάξις, from its military meaning—a
company of soldiers → expedition → journey
ὁ ἀφέντης < AG αὐθέντης—master
μπορῶ, ἐμπορῶ < AG εὐπορέω—find a way, be able
κερδίζω < AG ἐκέρδισα (aorist of κερδαίνω)—gain, win
iii) Adaptations from French:
ὁ κόντος = le comte (Latin *comes*)
κουγκεστήσει < noun κουγκουέστα = conquête, with the s of the
original root.

'Η Θυσία τοῦ Αβραάμ ' (*The Sacrifice of Abraham*)—Seventeenth
century AD
Although the name of the poet has not been handed down, it is most
probable that this religious drama in verse is the work of Vitsentzos
Kornaros and that he wrote it shortly before the *Erotocritos*. The drama
starts with the command delivered by the angel to Abraham that he

should sacrifice his only son and, as it progresses, it shows us the reactions of Abraham himself, Sarah and Isaac. Italian and French poets had already composed dramas with this subject but the Greek writer gave the story a more personal treatment. For example, when Abraham tries to wake Isaac up early, his son wants to be left to sleep longer as it is not yet time for school.

Ὤφου, ἀφεντάκι μου γλυκύ, κι ἄς μέ 'θελες ἀφήσει
καὶ μὲ τὴν ὥρα τοῦ σκολειοῦ ἐγώ 'θελα ξυπνήσει.

(493, 494)

Oh, father dear, if you would only leave me alone, I would still wake up in time for school.

Isaac is also worried that his mother has not dressed him as usual.

Ὁ λογισμός μου δὲ μπορεῖ κι ὁ νοῦς νὰ τὸ γροικήσῃ,
γιὰ ποιὰ ἀφορμὴ ἡ μάννα μου δὲν ἦρθε νὰ μὲ ντύσῃ.

(509, 510)

I really cannot understand why my mother has not come to dress me.

When they are up on the mountain and Isaac learns the truth, he finally consents to be sacrificed and asks for his father's blessing. Abraham is just about to bring down the knife, when the angel appears and Isaac is saved. They return to the house and to Sarah and the play ends with Abraham singing of the power of God.

The following extract is from the laments of Sarah, before Abraham goes to wake their son. She thinks of the happy past but cannot prevent her present grief from breaking in.

Ἐννιὰ μῆνες σ' ἐβάσταξα, τέκνο μου, κανακάρη,
    'ς τοῦτο τὸ κακορρίζικο καὶ σκοτεινὸ κουφάρι.
Τρεῖς χρόνους, γιέ μου, σοῦ 'διδα τὸ γάλα τῶ βυζῶ μου
    κ' ἐσύ 'σουνε τὰ μάτια μου κ' ἐσύ 'σουνε τὸ φῶς μου.
Ἐθώρουν κ' ἐμεγάλωνες ὡσὰ δεντροῦ κλωνάρι
    κ' ἐπλήθενες 'ς τὴν ἀρετή, 'ς τὴ γνώση καὶ 'ς τὴ
                                                        χάρη·
καὶ τώρα, 'πέ μου, ποιὰ χαρὰ βούλεσαι νὰ μοῦ δώσῃς;

45

σὰν ἀστραπὴ καὶ σὰ βροντή, θὲς νὰ χαθῆς, νὰ λειώσῃς.
Κ' ἐγὼ πῶς εἶναι μπορετὸ δίχως σου πλιὸ νὰ ζήσω;
ποιὸ θάρρος ἔχω, ποιὰ δροσά, 'ς τὰ γέρα μου τὰ πίσω;
Πόση χαρὰ τ' ἀντρόγυνον ἐπήραμεν ἀντάμι,
ὄντα μᾶς εἶπεν ὁ Θεὸς τὸ πῶς σὲ θέλω κάμει!
Καημένο σπίτι τ' Ἀβραάμ, πόσες χαρὲς ἐξώθης,
παιδάκι μ', ὄνταν ἔπεσες 'ς τὴ γῆ κ' ἐφανερώθης!
Πῶς ἐγυρίσαν οἱ χαρὲς σὲ θλῖψες 'ς μιὰν ἡμέρα!
πῶς ἐσκορπίσαν τὰ καλὰ σὰ νέφη 'ς τὸν ἀέρα!

(375–90)

For nine months I carried you in my womb, dear child, my darling son, here in this ill-fated, dark-caverned body of mine. For three years, my son, I gave you milk from my breasts and you were all the world to me. I watched you as you grew, like the branch of a tree, and you increased in virtue, in knowledge and in grace.

And now, tell me, what joy can you give me? For we are going to lose you and you will vanish, like a flash of lightning or a clap of thunder. And then, how can I live any more without you? What assurance or pleasure will I have left for my old age ahead?

What joy we felt, man and wife together, when the Lord told us that I was going to bear you! Unlucky house of Abraham, what happiness you brought to it when you made your appearance and were revealed to us!

How such joy has turned to sorrow in one day! How all our blessings have vanished like clouds into the air!

Ὁ Ἐρωτόκριτος τοῦ Βιτσέντζου Κορνάρου (*The Erotocritos of Vitsentzos Kornaros*)—Seventeenth century AD

The *Erotocritos* is a long poem of 10,052 lines, written in rhyming verse like the *Sacrifice of Abraham*. It is a love poem which sometimes becomes didactic when the poet pauses to address any reader who has known the trials of love.

κι ὅποιος τοῦ πόθου δούλεψε εἰσὲ καιρὸν κιανένα,
ἂς ἔρθῃ νὰ τ' ἀφουκραστῇ ὅ, τ' εἶναι ἐδῶ γραμμένα,
νὰ πάρῃ ξόμπλι κι ἀρμηνειὰ βαθιὰ νὰ θεμελιώνῃ
πάντα σ' ἀμάλαγη φιλιά, ὁποὺ νὰ μὴ κομπώνῃ·

A 11–14

Whoever has suffered at any time from desire, let him come and listen to these words, in order to equip himself with weapons and to stand firm against all the snares of unrelenting love.

The poem is set in Athens, but not in any specific historical period.

εἰς τὴν ᾿Αθήνα, πού 'τονε τσῆ μάθησης ἡ βρῶσις
καὶ τὸ θρονὶ τῆς ἀρετῆς κι ὁ πόταμος τσῆ γνώσης.

A 25–6

In Athens, the fount of learning, the throne of virtue and the river of knowledge.

The story concerns Aretousa, the only daughter of King Heracles, and Erotocritos, a courtier's son. Their unsuitable love certainly turns out to be an ' ἀμάλαγη φιλιά '. Erotocritos sings of his hopeless love every night and Aretousa conceives a passion for the singer she has never seen. Realising that he cannot hope to marry a princess, Erotocritos goes into self-imposed exile and during his absence Aretousa learns, by a chance discovery, the identity of the mysterious singer. On Erotocritos' return, which takes place because his father is ill, the two lovers meet regularly at a barred window of the palace, until the king, finding out about their love, orders Erotocritos out of the kingdom and arranges a marriage for Aretousa with a prince of Byzantium. Her refusal to marry the prince leads to an imprisonment for her which lasts until Erotocritos returns from abroad four years later. He comes in disguise as a warrior and distinguishes himself by making successful raids on the army of the Vlachs which is besieging Athens. He saves the king's life and wins a duel which decides victory for the Athenians. Erotocritos, therefore, is welcomed into the king's home but when he asks for the hand of the king's daughter in marriage, he is told that Aretousa refuses to marry anyone. The eventual recognition scene is lengthy but at last his true identity is revealed and a marriage is arranged. At this point the poet leaves the reader to draw his own conclusions.

The language of the poem is full of imagery and the style is formulaic and repetitive in the manner of epic. The Greek contains features peculiar to the Cretan dialect. For example the article τῆς τίς becomes τσῆ or τσί before a consonant and there is a tendency to insert a γ sound between vowels as is seen in the following:

γιατρεύγονται = ἰατρεύονται

παύγουσι = παύουσι

Leaving aside changes due to dialect, the language of the poem is remarkably pure, with very few foreign words.

The first extract is part of the speech of Aretousa's nurse who is comforting her by assuring her that time works wonders. This is a recurrent theme of the poem from its very first words, τοῦ κύκλου τὰ γυρίσματα. The second extract describes the dawn of the day on which Erotocritos will reveal himself to Aretousa.

1. Book III 1629–36

> Ἄφης τσὶ μέρες νὰ διαβοῦ, τὸ χρόνο νὰ περάσῃ,
> τ' ἄγρια θεριὰ μερώνουσι μὲ τὸν καιρὸ στὰ δάση.
> Μὲ τὸν καιρὸ τὰ δύσκολα καὶ τὰ βαρὰ ἀλαφραίνου,
> οἱ ἀνάγκες, πάθη κι ἀρρωστιὲς γιατρεύγουνται καὶ γιαίνου·
> μὲ τὸν καιρὸ οἱ ἀνεμικὲς κ' οἱ ταραχὲς σκολάζου,
> καὶ τὰ ζεστὰ κρυγαίνουσι, τὰ μαργωμένα βράζου·
> μὲ τὸν καιρὸ οἱ συννεφιὲς παύγουσι κ' οἱ ἀντάρες,
> κ' εὐκὲς μεγάλες γίνουνται μὲ τὸν καιρὸ οἱ κατάρες.

Let the days pass, let time go by. In time the wild creatures in the woods grow tame. In time the difficult and the heavy are made light; troubles, sufferings and ills are cured and made well. In time winds and turmoils abate and the hot grows cold and the frozen boils. In time storms and clouds clear and curses, in time, become great prayers.

2. Book V 767–96

> Ἦρθεν ἡ ὥρα κι ὁ καιρὸς κ' ἡ μέρα ξημερώνει
> νὰ φανερώσῃ ὁ Ρώκριτος τὸ πρόσωπο, ποὺ χώνει.
> Ἐφάνη ὁλόχαρη ἡ αὐγὴ καὶ τὴ δροσούλα ρίχνει,
> σημάδια τῆς ξεφάντωσης κείνη τὴν ὥρα δείχνει.
> Χορτάρια βγήκασι στὴ γῆς, τὰ δεντρουλάκια ἀθίσα,
> κι ἀπὸ τς ἀγκάλες τ' οὐρανοῦ γλυκὺς βορρᾶς ἐφύσα,
> τὰ περιγιάλια λάμπασι, κ' ἡ θάλασσα κοιμᾶτο,
> γλυκὺς σκοπὸς εἰς τὰ δεντρὰ κ' εἰς τὰ νερὰ γροικᾶτο·
> ὁλόχαρη καὶ λαμπιρὴ ἡ μέρα ξημερώνει,
> ἐγέλαν ἡ 'Ανατολή, κ' ἡ Δύσι καμαρώνει.
> Ὁ Ἥλιος τὶς ἀκτῖνές του παρὰ ποτὲ στολίζει
> μὲ λάψι, κι ὅλα τὰ βουνιὰ καὶ κάμπους ὀμορφίζει.

Χαμοπετώντας τὰ πουλιὰ ἐγλυκοκιλαηδοῦσα,
στὰ κλωναράκια τῶ δεντρῶ ἐσμῖγαν· κ' ἐφιλοῦσα,
δυὸ δυὸ ἐζευγαρώνασι, ζεστὸς καιρὸς ἐκίνα,
ἔσμιξες, γάμους καὶ χαρὲς ἐδείχνασιν κ' ἐκεῖνα·
ἐσκόρπισεν ἡ συννεφιά, οἱ ἀντάρες ἐχαθῆκα,
πολλὰ σημάδια τσῆ χαρᾶς στὸν οὐρανὸ φανῆκα·
παρὰ ποτέ ντως λαμπιρὰ τριγύρου στολισμένα
στὸν οὐρανόν 'ν' τὰ νέφαλα σὰν παραχρυσωμένα.
Τὰ πάθη μπλιὸ δὲν κιλαηδεῖ τὸ πρικαμένο ἀηδόνι,
ἀμὴ πετᾶ πασίχαρο, μ' ἄλλα πουλιὰ σιμώνει.
Γελοῦν τσῆ χώρας τὰ στενά, κ' οἱ στράτες καμαρώνου,
ὅλα γροικοῦν κουρφὲς χαρές, κι ὅλα τσὶ φανερώνου·
καὶ μέσ' στὴ σκοτεινὴ φλακή, πού 'τον ἡ 'Αρετοῦσα,
ἐμπῆκα δυὸ ὄμορφα πουλιὰ κ' ἐγλυκοκιλαηδοῦσα·
στὴν κεφαλὴ τῆς 'Αρετῆς συχνιὰ χαμοπετοῦσι,
καὶ φαίνεταί σου καὶ χαρὲς μεγάλες προμηνοῦσι·
πάλι μὲ τὸν κιλαηδισμὸν ἐκ τὴ φλακὴν ἐφύγα,
ἀγκαλιαστὰ περιμπλεκτὰ τσὶ μουρές τως ἐσμῖγα.

So dawned the day and came the hour and time for Erotocritos to shed his long disguise. Full of joy the dawn appeared and scattered the dew and at that early hour gave signs of joy ahead. The earth turned green and the young trees blossomed and from heaven's embrace there blew a mild north wind. The shores shone and the sea slept and a sweet refrain sounded in the trees and in the deep.

So dawned the day, full of joy and bright; the East laughed and the West stood proudly by. The sun more than ever endowed its rays with light and spread beauty over all the hills and plains.

Flying low the birds sang sweetly and met and courted in the branches. Two by two they paired off, roused by the heat. Meetings, marriages and delights they too were proclaiming.

The cloudy sky cleared and the storms subsided; and many signs of joy could be seen in the heavens. More brightly decked all round than ever before were the clouds above, all clad in gold.

No more did the sad swallow utter its laments but it flew, full of joy, to meet with other birds. The country's passes laughed and the roads stood proud; all heard the secret joy and all proclaimed it.

And into the dark cell where Aretousa lay there flew two beautiful birds, singing sweetly, flying low back and forth over Aretousa's head. And they too, clearly, were proclaiming great joy. Then with the same bird song they left the cell and, embracing and entwined, they laid their heads together.

At the end of the poem Kornaros reveals his own identity.

3. Book V 1539–1548

Θωρῶ πολλοὺς καὶ πεθυμοῦ, κ' ἔχω το γροικημένα,
νὰ μάθουν τίς ἐκόπιασε εἰς τ' ἀπανωγραμμένα,
κ' ἐγὼ δὲ θὲ νὰ κουρφευτῶ, κι ἀγνώριστο νὰ μ' ἔχου,
μὰ θέλω νὰ φανερωθῶ, κι ὅλοι νὰ μὲ κατέχου.
Βιτζέντζος εἶν' ὁ ποιητὴς κ' εἰς τὴ γενιὰ Κορνάρος,
ποὺ νὰ βρεθῇ ἀκριμάτιστος, ὄντε τὸν πάρῃ ὁ χάρος.
Στὴ Στείαν ἐγεννήθηκε, στὴ Στείαν ἐνεθράφη,
ἐκεῖ 'καμε κ' ἐκόπιασε ἐτοῦτα, ποὺ σᾶς γράφει.
Στὸ Κάστρον ἐπαντρεύτηκε, σὰν ἀρμηνεύγ' ἡ φύσι·
τὸ τέλος του ἔχει νὰ γενῇ, ὅπου ὁ Θεὸς ὁρίσῃ.

I have heard it said that many people want to know who it is that has laboured to write this poem. I have no wish to hide away and remain unknown. I should like to reveal myself for everyone to know who I am.

The poet's name is Vitsentzos of the family of Kornaros. May he be found free from sin when Death comes to take him! He was born and bred in Siteia and that is where he worked to produce what you read here. He got married in Herakleion when the time was ripe. His end has still to come, when God decides.

Grammatical Points and vocabulary from Ἡ Θυσία τοῦ Ἀβραάμ and Ὁ Ἐρωτόκριτος
i) ἡμέρες > μέρες
ἡμερώνω > μερώνω
ἐκείνη > κείνη
εἰς τὰ δάση > στὰ δάση

These changes indicate the loss of an unaccented initial vowel. This tendency also explains how οὐδέν became δέν (not), how αὐτόν, αὐτούς became τόν, τούς etc., and how εἰς τὸν became στὸν, εἰς τὴν became στὴν etc. Some other examples of the formation of modern Greek words in this way are:

ὀμμάτιον > μάτι (eye)
ὀσπίτιον > σπίτι (house)
ὀψάριον > ψάρι (fish)
ἐρωτῶ > ρωτῶ (ask)
εὐρίσκω > βρίσκω (find)

Note that the famous ηὕρηκα of Archimedes would be βρῆκα in modern Greek, the same word but subject to pronunciation change and the loss of the first syllable.

Apart from the changes which have become well established in modern Greek, the same principle of the possible loss or interchange of the vowel in an unstressed initial syllable gives rise to a vast array of variations in the different dialects of Greek. The following are a few examples from *Erotocritos*:

ἀλαφραίνου for ἐλαφραίνου (ἐλαφρῶνουν)
πεθυμοῦ for ἐπιθυμοῦν
Στείαν for Σητείαν
φλακή for φυλακή
ἀρμηνεύγει for ἐρμηνεύει

ii) Many nouns and adjectives changed as a result of the pronunciation of ε or ι with a following vowel as a single syllable. For example, καρδία became καρδιά (heart) and χωρίον became χωριό (village). Examples from the passages are:

ἐννέα > ἐννιά (both forms are still found today)
πλέον > πλιό (MG—πιό)
θερία (AG θηρία) > θεριά
ἀρρωστίες > ἀρρωστιές (but MG ἀρρώστιες)
βαρέα > βαρά (βαριά)

Some dialects of modern Greek still preserve the old forms.

As a result of such synizesis the ancient Greek third declension adjectives of the type βαθύς βαθεία βαθύ became βαθύς βαθιά βαθύ.

iii) Some other features of dialectical variation include the rearrangement of sounds within a word, the loss of a final –ν and simple changes or omissions of vowels or consonants.

πρικαμένο = πικραμένο	κουρφές = κρυφές
κουρφευτῶ = κρυφτῶ	δέντρον = δένδρον
εὐκή = εὐχή	σκολάζου(ν) = σχολάζου(ν)
λάψι = λάμψη	ἄθισα(ν) = ἄνθισα(ν)
βουνιά = βουνά	συχνιά = συχνά
τως, ντως = τους (gen. pl.)	

51

σκολάζου, βράζου, ἐχάθηκα, ἔφυγα, τῶ βυζῶ, τῶ δεντρῶ have all lost their final –ν.

iv) οἱ was substituted for αἱ by this time in the feminine nominative plural of the article, by analogy with the plural forms of nouns which became largely common for masculine and feminine. Thus in the passages are found οἱ χαρές, οἱ ἀνάγκες, οἱ ταραχές, οἱ συννεφιές, οἱ ἀντάρες and οἱ στράτες etc.

v) τοί = τίς. τίς became the regular feminine accusative plural of the article as in τὶς ἡμέρες, τὶς ἀκτῖνες, τοὶ μοῦρες.

vi) Two forms of the third person plural of the present tense are found in use at the same time during this period. This is a transitional characteristic; the –ουν ending is regular in modern Greek. Examples from the passages include: μερώνουσι, κρυγαίνουσι, χαμοπετοῦσι, προμηνοῦσι, and ἀλαφραί νου(ν), βράζου(ν), καμαρώνου(ν), φανερώνου(ν).

vii) Third declension nouns of the type φύσις φύσεως are found with the following simplifications:

  ἡ φύσι for ἡ φύσις
  μὲ λάψι for μὲ λάμψιν
  τῆς ξεφάντωσης for τῆς ξεφαντώσεως

In modern Greek the form of this type of noun has now been standardised as follows:

	singular	plural
nominative	ἡ σκέψη	οἱ σκέψεις
accusative	τὴ σκέψη	τὶς σκέψεις
genitive	τῆς σκέψης	τῶν σκέψεων

viii) The relative pronoun is πού or ὁπού, as in:

  εἰς τὴν Αθήνα, πού 'τονε τοῆ μάθησης ἡ βρῶσις
    (in Athens which is the fount of learning)
  τὸ πρόσωπο πού χώνει
    (the 'persona' which he is hiding)
  ἐτοῦτα πού σᾶς γράφει
    (this which he is writing for you)

The relative pronoun of ancient Greek ὅς or ὅστις has been replaced by ὅπου (ὁπού) or πού. In more formal speech in modern Greek ὁ ὁποῖος is used. ὅπου and πού are indeclinable. They are also still used in their original sense of 'where' or sometimes 'when', as in the last line of the poet's concluding words about himself:

τὸ τέλος του ἔχει νὰ γενῇ, ὅπου ὁ θεὸς ὁρίσῃ.

His end has still to come, when God decides.

ix) The vocabulary of Vitsentzos Kornaros is largely classical with a few Venetian or Latin derivations, many of which later came into frequent use in Greek. Some interesting developments are shown below:
From ancient Greek:

ὡσά(ν)(= like) (also σάν) < ὡς ἂν
ἀντάμι (MG ἀντάμα)(= together) < ἐντάμα < ἐν τῷ ἅμα
περιγιάλι (= sea-shore) < παραγιάλιν < παρ' αἰγιαλόν
ξημερώνει (= day breaks) < ἐξημερώνει (ἐκ + ἡμέρα)
παντρεύω (= I marry) < πανδρεύω < ὑπ-ανδρ-εύω < AG ὕπανδρος
(under a man, married)
χορτάρι (=grass) —diminutive of χόρτος (grass or hay)
ἴντα (ἰντά) (= τί (what?)) This word is still used in the modern Cypriot dialect. The form originated from τί εἶν(αι) τα (τὸ);
ὅντα (ὅντε, ὅντας) (= when) < ὅταν
ἀμή (ἀμέ, ἀμά) (= but) < ἂν μή

From Latin:

κάμπος—plain < 'campus'
στράτα—road < 'strata'—paved (way)

It is in this period that rhyme first occurs, a Western element which is not found in the older demotic songs of the mainland. From the *Sacrifice of Abraham* and the *Erotocritos* we can see that the poet has an easy mastery of rhyming couplets. Many of these couplets are still sung in Crete today and have become part of the Cretans' repertoire of '**mantinades**'. The word is Venetian and its literal meaning is 'morning songs' but, for the Cretans, the mantinades are lively rhymes on a wide variety of themes. The following four couplets are from a twentieth century collection and are given here to show the continuity of this type of verse.

Κρήτη, μητέρα τσ' ἀρχοντιᾶς,˜ τῆς λευτεριᾶς δασκάλα
ποὺ γράφετ' ἡ ἱστορία σου κάθε φορὰ μὲ μπάλα.

Κρήτη, πῶς εἶσ' ἀρχόντισσα τὸ δείχνουν τὰ βουνά σου

θεριὰ σὲ πολεμήσανε μὰ πέσανε μπροστά σου.

Τὴ λευτεριὰ ἐστήριξες, κι ἂς μάθει ὅποιος δὲν ξέρει,
στὸ τιμημένο ὅπλο σου τὸ Κρητικὸ μαχαίρι.

Σκλάβος δὲν ζῆ ὁ Κρητικός, τὸ ξέρουν κι οἱ ἐχθροί μας
γιατὶ 'χομε πολιτισμὸ παλιὸ μέσ' τὴν ψυχή μας.[19]

Crete, mother of distinction, mistress of freedom;
Always in bullets is your story written.

Crete, your mountains show what a grand lady you are;
Wild beasts fought you but always fell before you.

You have upheld freedom, let all hear it said,
And your worthy weapon was the Cretan blade.

The Cretan is no slave, our enemies know this well;
Memories of an ancient past within us proudly dwell.

The Cypriots have a similar type of verse composed by singers known as 'pyitarides'. A good discussion of them and of the Cretan singers is to be found in Roderick Beaton's *Folk Poetry of Modern Greece*.[20]

The metre of most of the verse which has preceded and of the demotic songs which follow is the fifteen-syllable verse which became the normal medium for demotic Greek poetry. Sometimes referred to as 'political verse', this metre had come into frequent use as early as the tenth century AD when some change from classical metres was necessary because of the change to a stress accent in Greek. The line falls into two units which allows for various patterns of repetition or parallel expressions, as will be seen clearly in the poems which follow.

Τὰ Δημοτικὰ Τραγούδια *(Demotic Songs)*

These songs are the work of ordinary people. Anyone could and did 'make a song' and in popular literature poetry was the normal medium. The songs of the demotic tradition do not use rhyme but, as in all oral poetry, there are constantly recurring features, both repetitions within the same song and variations on standard formulae which are common to the whole tradition. For example, in the lines quoted below a question is immediately followed by its answer which is mainly repetition.

Ὁ Ὄλυμπος κι ὁ Κίσαβος, τὰ δυὸ βουνὰ μαλώνουν,
τὸ ποιὸ νὰ ῥίξη τὴ βροχή, τὸ ποιὸ νὰ ῥίξη χιόνι.
Ὁ Κίσαβος ῥίχνει τὴ βροχὴ κι ὁ Ὄλυμπος τὸ χιόνι.

(Extract 1 1–3)

[Γιατὶ εἶναι μαῦρα τὰ βουνὰ καὶ στέκουν βουρκωμένα;]
μὴν ἄνεμος τὰ πολεμᾶ, μήνα βροχὴ τὰ δέρνει;
Κι οὐδ᾽ ἄνεμος τὰ πολεμᾶ κι οὐδὲ βροχὴ τὰ δέρνει.

(Extract 3 1–3)

A key word or phrase may be repeated constantly, as in τὰ μικρὰ παιδόπουλα or τὰ τρυφερὰ παιδόπουλα in the third extract. Also, because of the pattern of the fifteen-syllable line, the second half of the line can be made to echo or contrast with the first half.

κάθε κορφὴ καὶ φλάμπουρο, κάθε κλαδὶ καὶ κλέφτης.

(Extract 1 line 9)

Κι ὁ Θοδωράκης μίλησε, κι ὁ Θοδωράκης λέει·

(Extract 2 line 12)

This last line is also an example of a past tense being followed by a present tense which is common to many poems:

e.g. Καὶ τοῦ Γιαννάκη μίλησε καὶ τοῦ Γιαννάκη λέει

And he spoke to Jannakis and says to him...[21]

In the whole body of the folk songs there are certain recurring motifs, such as a bird, or often three birds, who brings news and sits on a rock and sings, like the eagle in the first extract who sits on a rock and speaks to the sun:

πάνω στὴν πέτρα κάθεται καὶ μὲ τὸν ἥλιο λέει·

(line 13)

There are many formulaic phrases relating to numbers. In a famous song about the bridge of Arta we read of:

σαράντα πέντε μάστοροι καὶ ἑξήντα μαθητᾶδες

Forty-five craftsmen and sixty apprentices

In another poem there are:

σαράντα πέντε Κυριακὲς κι ἑξηνταδυὸ Δευτέρες

Forty-five Sundays and sixty-two Mondays[21]

Similarly, in the first extract Olympus says

ἔχω σαράντα δυὸ κορφὲς κι ἑξήντα δυὸ βρυσούλες

(line 8)

In the second extract the Klephts wear

τὶς πέντε ἀράδες τὰ κουμπιά, τὶς ἔξι τὰ τσαπράζια

(line 4)

The poet's skill lay in the imaginative use of the formulae and in balancing the rhythm of his lines. He would also make use of much imagery from and personification of the world of nature. In the first extract the mountains Olympus and Kisavos are cleverly personified and in the third extract the description of mountains as βουρκωμένα, 'covered in rainclouds', also brings to mind its other meaning of 'brimming with tears'.

The first two poems are songs of the Klephts. In the first, Mount Olympus prides itself on being the hiding place of the Klephts. The second poem is more closely related to actual events. In January 1806 the Sultan had issued a 'firman' ordering the rounding up of the band of Klephts led by Theodorus Kolokotronis in the Peloponnese. The poem relates the advice given by Kolokotronis to his followers that they should flee for safety. In fact, they refused to obey him and the band resisted for a further three months. The third poem is taken from everyday life. The conception of death as Charon was familiar and joking in the face of death was common.[22]

1. Olympus and Kisavos—The Battle of the Mountains

Ὁ Ὄλυμπος κι ὁ Κίσαβος, τὰ δυὸ βουνὰ μαλώνουν,
τὸ ποιὸ νὰ ρίξη τὴ βροχή, τὸ ποιὸ νὰ ρίξη χιόνι.
Ὁ Κίσαβος ρίχνει βροχή κι ὁ Ὄλυμπος τὸ χιόνι.

56

Γυρίζει τότ' ὁ Ὄλυμπος καὶ λέγει τοῦ Κισάβου·
"Μὴ μὲ μαλώνης, Κίσαβε, μπρὲ τουρκοπατημένε,
ποὺ σὲ πατάει ἡ Κονιαριὰ κι οἱ Λαρσινοὶ ἀγάδες.
Ἐγὼ εἶμ' ὁ γέρος Ὄλυμπος στὸν κόσμο ξακουσμένος,
ἔχω σαράντα δυὸ κορφὲς κι ἐξήντα δυὸ βρυσοῦλες,
κάθε κορφὴ καὶ φλάμπουρο, κάθε κλαδὶ καὶ κλέφτης.
Κι ὅταν τὸ παίρν' ἡ ἄνοιξη κι ἀνοίγουν τὰ κλαδάκια,
γεμίζουν τὰ βουνὰ κλεφτιὰ καὶ τὰ λαγκάδια σκλάβους.
Ἔχω καὶ τὸ χρυσὸν ἀιτό, τὸ χρυσοπλουμισμένο,
πάνω στὴν πέτρα κάθεται καὶ μὲ τὸν ἥλιο λέγει·
'ἥλιε μ', δὲν κροῦς τ' ἀποταχύ, μόν' κροῦς τὸ μεσημέρι,
νὰ ζεσταθοῦν τὰ νύχια μου, τὰ νυχοπόδαρά μου' "

Olympus and Kisavos, the two mountains, are quarrelling: which of them is to pour down rain and which to send snow. Kisavos pours rain and Olympus sends snow; Olympus then turns to Kisavos and says to him: 'Do not abuse me, Kisavos. You are under the heel of the Turks, you are trampled by the hordes from Iconium, the lords of Larisa. I am ancient Olympus, famous throughout the world; I have forty-two peaks and sixty-two sweet springs. On every peak a flag flies; behind each branch stands a klepht. When spring comes and the young branches bloom, the mountains fill with klephts, but the valleys are filled with slaves. And mine is the golden eagle, the bird of golden plumage; he sits upon a rock and cries out to the sun: "My sun, your shafts do not hit me at dawn: they only reach me at noon, to warm my claws, to warm my taloned feet" '.

'the hordes from Iconium' (Κονιαριά)—a group of Turks who settled in Thessaly and Southern Macedonia.

2. Kolokotronis' Band

Λάμπουν τὰ χιόνια στὰ βουνὰ κι ὁ ἥλιος στὰ λαγκάδια,
λάμπουν καί τ' ἀλαφρὰ σπαθιὰ τῶν Κολοκοτρωναίων,
πόχουν τ' ἀσήμια τὰ πολλά, τὶς ἀσημένιες πάλες,
τὶς πέντε ἀράδες τὰ κουμπιά, τὶς ἔξι τὰ τσαπράζια,
ὁποὺ δὲν καταδέχονται τὴ γῆς νὰ τὴν πατήσουν.
Καβάλα τρῶνε τὸ ψωμί, καβάλα πολεμᾶνε,
καβάλα πᾶν στὴν ἐκκλησιά, καβάλα προσκυνᾶνε,
καβάλα παίρν' ἀντίδερο ἀπ' τοῦ παπᾶ τὸ χέρι.

Φλωριὰ ῥίχνουν στὴν Παναγιά, φλωριὰ ῥίχνουν στοὺς ἅγιους,
καὶ στὸν ἀφέντη τὸ Χριστὸ τὶς ἀσημένιες πάλες.
"Χριστέ μας, βλόγα τὰ σπαθιά, βλόγα μας καὶ τὰ χέρια."
Κι ὁ Θοδωράκης μίλησε, κι ὁ Θοδωράκης λέει·
"τοῦτ' οἱ χαρὲς ποὺ κάνουμε σὲ λύπη θὰ μᾶς
βγάλουν.
Ἀπόψ' εἶδα στὸν ὕπνο μου, στὴν ὑπνοφαντασιά μου,
θολὸ ποτάμι πέρναγα καὶ πέρα δὲν ἐβγῆκα.
Ἐλᾶτε νὰ σκορπίσουμε, μπουλούκια νὰ γενοῦμε.
Σύρε, Γιῶργο μ', στὸν τόπο σου, Νικήτα, στὸ Λοντάρι·
ἐγὼ πάου στὴν Καρύταινα, πάου στοὺς ἐδικούς μου,
ν' ἀφήκω τὴ διαθήκη μου καὶ τὶς παραγγολές μου,
τὶ θὰ περάσω θάλασσα, στὴ Ζάκυνθο θὰ πάω."

Snow flashes on the hills, sunshine in the valleys, and the swift swords of the men of Kolokotronis flash. They have much silver, and bullets made of silver; they wear five rows of [silver] buttons, and six of silver decorations. They never deign to tread the earth. Mounted upon their horses they eat their food, mounted they fight, mounted they go to church; mounted they worship, and mounted they take the holy bread from the priest's hand. They offer gold coins to our Lady, gold coins to the saints, and to Christ, our Lord, silver bullets. 'Christ bless our swords, and bless our hands.' And Theodore spoke, and Theodore said: 'This feast we hold will lead to sorrow. Last night I saw in my sleep, in my dream, that I was trying to cross a muddy stream and did not get across. Come, let us disperse, let us break into different bands. George, you go to your homeland, and you, Niketas, to Leontari; I am going to Karytena, to my people, to make my will and give my orders, for I shall cross the sea and go to Zante.

3. The Passing of Death

Γιατὶ εἶναι μαῦρα τὰ βουνὰ καὶ στέκουν βουρκωμένα;
μὴν ἄνεμος τὰ πολεμᾶ, μήνα βροχὴ τὰ δέρνει;
Κι οὐδ ἄνεμος τὰ πολεμᾶ κι οὐδὲ βροχὴ τὰ δέρνει,
μόνε διαβαίνει ὁ Χάροντας μὲ τοὺς ἀποθαμένους.
Σέρνει τοὺς νιοὺς ἀπὸ μπροστά, τοὺς γέροντες κατόπι,
τὰ τρυφερὰ παιδόπουλα στὴ σέλα ἀραδιασμένα.
Παρακαλοῦν οἱ γέροντες, κι οἱ νέοι γονατίζουν,
καὶ τὰ μικρὰ παιδόπουλα τὰ χέρια σταυρωμένα·

"Χάρε μου, διάβ' ἀπὸ χωριό, κάτσε σὲ κρύα βρύση,
νὰ πιοῦν οἱ γέροντες νερό, κι οἱ νιοὶ νὰ λιθαρίσουν,
καὶ τὰ μικρὰ παιδόπουλα λουλούδια νὰ μαζώζουν. "
—"'Ανὶ διαβῶν ἀπὸ χωριό, ἄν ἀπὸ κρύα βρύση,
ἔρχονται οἱ μάνες γιὰ νερό, γνωρίζουν τὰ παιδιά τους,
γνωρίζονται τ' ἀντρόγενα καὶ χωρισμὸ δὲν ἔχουν. "

Why are the mountains black? Why do they stand covered in cloud? Is the wind fighting with them? Is the rain beating on them? Neither does the wind fight with them, nor does the rain beat upon them; it is Death who strides across them carrying away the dead. He drags the young in front of him, the old people behind, and the little tender children he carries in a row in his saddle. The old implore him, the young kneel before him, and the little children, with crossed arms, cry:

'Death, pass through a village, stop at a cool fountain for the old to drink the water, the young to play quoits, and the little children to gather flowers.'

'Should I go past a village, or by a cool fountain, the mothers come to fetch water and they will recognise their children; husbands and wives will recognise one another and it is hard to part them.'

Grammatical Points from Τὰ Δημοτικὰ Τραγούδια
Most of the features of modern Greek are now well established. The -ουν ending of the present tense predominates and all prepositions are followed by the accusative case, as in στὸν κόσμο, μὲ τὸν ἥλιο, ἀπὸ τὸ χέρι, γιὰ (διὰ) νερὸ and μὲ τοὺς ἀποθαμένους.

ποὺ is now regularly in use for the relative pronoun. To distinguish its use for an oblique case, a pronoun is often attached to the verb of the relative clause, as in ποὺ σὲ πατάει ἡ Κονιαρά where the antecedent 'you' is expressed by σέ (accusative case) inside the relative clause. Two further examples of this construction in modern Greek are:

τοὺς νέους ποὺ τοὺς εἴδαμε—the young people whom we saw
ὁ φίλος ποὺ τοῦ ἔδωσα τὰ βιβλία—the friend to whom I gave the
books

ii) The future tense is expressed by θὰ and the subjunctive, as in θὰ μᾶς βγάλουν, θὰ περάσω and θὰ πάω. The form θὰ has developed as follows:

θέλει ἵνα > θέλει νὰ > θενὰ > θὰ

With the present subjunctive it refers to what will be done continually, habitually or often. With the aorist subjunctive, as in all the examples here, it refers to what will happen at a specific time.

θὰ is also used with the imperfect indicative in a conditional sense.

e.g. ἂν δὲν τὸν γνώριζα καλά, δὲν θὰ τὸν πίστευα

If I had not known him well, I would not have believed him *or* If I did not know him well, I would not believe him.

iii) The use of να as the equivalent of ἵνα, introducing a purpose clause, has already been mentioned (page 44) and it is used regularly here as in νὰ ζεσταθοῦν τὰ νύχια μου and ἐλᾶτε νὰ σκορπίσουμε. It is also used for a deliberative question, as in μαλώνουν τὸ ποιὸ νὰ ῥίξη τὴ βροχή, and to replace an ancient Greek infinitive, as in δὲν καταδέχονται τῆς γῆς νὰ τὴν πατήσουν.

In the extracts given in the previous chapter we found the ancient Greek infinitive still in use but we see here that it has been phased out and replaced very largely by ἵνα or νὰ and the subjunctive. There is no infinitive in modern Greek. 'I want to work' is θέλω νὰ δουλέψω; 'I cannot go' is δὲν μπορῶ νὰ πάω.

Vocabulary from Τὰ Δημοτικὰ Τραγούδια

i) Vowel changes continue to occur in unstressed syllables:

ἀλαφρά = ἐλαφρά	light
ἀντίδερο = ἀντίδωρον	holy bread, Host
πάου = πάω	go
νιούς = νέους	the young

ii) Loss of an initial unstressed vowel:

βλογῶ < εὐλογῶ—to bless
μιλῶ < ὁμιλῶ—to speak
βγάλω < ἐβγάλλω < ἐκβάλλω—to throw out
βγαίνω < ἐβγαίνω < ἐκβαίνω—to go out

iii) Words formed with the endings –νω, –ίζω, –άζω:

δέρνω < AG δέρω—to beat
παίρνω < AG ἐπ-αίρω—to take
περνῶ < AG περάω—to cross
ῥίχνω < AG ῥίπτω—to throw
γονατίζω < AG γονατ– (knee)—to kneel
γυρίζω < AG γῦρος (circle)—to turn
πλουμίζω < Latin 'pluma' (feather)—to feather
ἀραδιάζω < Venetian 'arada' (furrow)—to set in rows

iv) Words formed through the diminutive :
From ancient Greek:

τὸ σπαθί (sword) < τὸ σπάθιον, diminutive of ἡ σπάθη
τὸ ψωμί (bread) < τὸ ψωμίον, diminutive of ὁ ψωμός (morsel, scrap of meat or bread)
τὸ κλαδί (branch) < τὸ κλαδίον, diminutive of ὁ κλάδος
τὸ ποτάμι (river) < τὸ ποτάμιον, diminutive of ὁ ποταμός

From Latin:

τὸ φλωρί (florin) < τὸ φλωρίον (dim.) < 'florinus'
τὸ φλάμπουρο (flag) < τὸ φλάμπουλον < φλάμμουλον < flammūlum (little flame; flame-coloured flag)

v) Words derived from other languages:
Turkish—ὁ ἀγᾶς—aga, chief officer
    τὰ τσαπράζια—silver decorations of waistcoat (capraz)
    μπουλούκι—band (of warriors) (bölük)
Venetian—ἀράδα—row (arada—furrow) (Latin—arare—to plough)
Latin—καβάλα—on horseback (caballus—horse)
    σέλα—saddle (sella—seat, chair)
Albanian—λουλοῦδι—flower
vi) Miscellaneous:
    σκλάβος < Σλαβηνός—Slav (used from the eighth century AD to denote a slave or a prisoner-of-war)
    μπρέ < μ' ρέ < μωρέ (fool! child!)—unceremonious form of address
    ἀπόψε < ἀπ' ὄψε—late in the day
The –πουλος suffix, as in παιδόπουλο, is a diminutive and comes from the Latin 'pullus'—a young animal. (It is a common surname ending in modern Greek, literally having the sense of 'son of' e.g. Μιχαλόπουλος—son of Michael.)
vii) Compound Words:
    τουρκοπατημένος—trodden by the Turk
    χρυσοπλουμισμένος—golden-feathered
    νυχοπόδαρα—taloned feet
    ὑπνοφαντασία—dream (in sleep)
    ἀντρόγενο (MG ἀντρόγυννον)—husband and wife, married couple
The first four examples are determinative compounds where the first

element explains the second. These are extremely numerous in Greek. Some examples from present-day Greek are:

τὸ πεζοδρόμιον—road for pedestrians, pavement

τὸ ξενοδοχεῖον—place (container) for visitors, hotel

ὁ σιδηρόδρομος—iron road, railway.

This word, as many others, is from Greek elements but is a copy of a foreign compound. Thus, one finds 'chemin de fer' in French, 'железная дорога' (jeleznaya doroga) in Russian and 'eisenbahn' in German.

The final example, ἀντρόγενο, is an example of a compound where the two parts would normally be linked with 'and' in translation. Examples from present-day Greek are:

Σαββατοκύριακο—Saturday and Sunday, weekend

πηγαινοερχόμενος—going and coming, going back and forth

αὐγολέμονο—egg and lemon (a soup or sauce)

μαχαιροπήρουνα—knife and fork, cutlery

From a period covering so many centuries and geographical areas it has been difficult to select only a few examples of Greek literature. It should be clear, however, that the Greek language was alive and thriving throughout these years of change. This is no surprise if one considers that the language of the church was Greek and that much of the administration of the Ottoman Empire was in the hands of Greeks. It is important to remember that the concept of what is Greek cannot be confined to what we think of as Greece today. This chapter has highlighted some areas of Greek-speaking populations over a period of five hundred years. The next chapter will describe the establishment of the frontiers of a political state called Greece. Many Greek speakers, or Hellenes to give a more precise description, did and still do live outside these frontiers.

CHAPTER FOUR

INDEPENDENCE AND THE FORMATION OF
A NATIONAL LANGUAGE
NINETEENTH AND TWENTIETH CENTURIES

At the beginning of the nineteenth century the Greeks began the fight for their independence but there was no single plan for war. Both inside and outside Greece there were patriots wanting to liberate their country from Ottoman rule. One such patriot, but only one of many, was **Rhigas Pheraios** (1757–98) who had served under the Phanariot Hospodars of Moldavia and Wallachia. He had worked in various central European cities including Vienna where he was known for his literary activities and his democratic idea for the creation of a multi-racial Balkan State with a predominantly Greek culture. He was eventually arrested by the Austrians for belonging to a conspiratorial organisation and was handed over to the Turks, who put him to death, but his name has lived on and his best known work today is his *War Hymn*:

Ὡς πότε, παλικάρια, νὰ ζοῦμεν στὰ στενά,
μονάχοι, σὰν λεοντάρια, στὲς ράχες, στὰ βουνά;
σπηλιὲς νὰ κατοικοῦμεν, νὰ βλέπωμεν κλαδιά;
Νὰ φεύγωμεν τὸν κόσμον γιὰ τὴν πικρὴν σκλαβιά;
ν' ἀφήνωμεν ἀδέλφια, πατρίδα καὶ γονεῖς,
τοὺς φίλους, τὰ παιδιά μας κι ὅλους τοὺς συγγενεῖς;
Καλύτερα μιᾶς ὥρας ἐλεύθερη ζωή,
παρὰ σαράντα χρόνων σκλαβιὰ καὶ φυλακή.

How long, young men, must we live in confinement, alone like lions on ridges in the hills? How long must we live in caves and look out on branches, shunning the world for bitter enslavement, leaving our land, brothers, parents, friends, our children and all our relations?
Better one hour of life that is free than forty years in slavery!

(First verse of two)

The Phanariots and the leaders of the Church hoped for a gradual development towards independence, using the considerable power which they already held under the Turks, but certain educated Greek scholars and merchants, at home and abroad, wanted more positive action. In 1814 a group of three Greek merchants in Russia founded a secret society in Odessa known as the Φιλικὴ Ἑταιρεία which began to plot the liberation of Greece and built up a network of communication with many patriots within Greece itself. Moreover, on the sea, many of the Greek islanders, to whom the Turks had entrusted the conduct of maritime commerce, had grown rich and powerful, particularly with the increase in trade which the continental blockade had brought them during the Napoleonic Wars. They had a tradition of independence and they too were ready to play a crucial role in the fighting.

At the same time, the Ottoman Empire was under strain at many points. Local 'pashas' were pursuing independent policies, even to the point of open rebellion as in the case of Ali Pasha, the Albanian governor at Ioannina, and the Empire was also involved in hostilities with several of her neighbours.

When the Greeks rose in revolt against the Turks in 1821, they did so by sporadic acts of rebellion rather than by a single concerted plan. The Φιλικὴ Ἑταιρεία was behind the initial planning, but where rebellion was sustained, it was wholly on the strength of local initiative. In the Peloponnese, in the mainland north of Corinth, known as Roumeli, and in certain islands there began a bloodthirsty period with gains and losses on both sides, not to mention terrible atrocities. From 1822 onwards, while the fighting continued, attempts were made to form a National Assembly but there were constant internal quarrels. Luckily the Turks did not have the manpower to inflict any decisive defeat until the arrival of Ibrahim Pasha in 1825 and the Greeks had certain distinct advantages such as skill at sea and experience of guerrilla fighting in their own difficult terrain. One further advantage for Greece lay in the sympathy of many Western liberals. Many individual Philhellenes had raised money for Greece and some had come to share in the fighting. When Byron came to Greece in 1824, he was bringing with him the first instalment of a loan from the London Committee of Philhellenes. It took the European governments much longer to give their support. Having recently defeated Napoleon and his liberal ideas, they had agreed at the Congress of Vienna to co-operate in preserving the existing order throughout Europe, including even the Ottoman Empire. When England, France and Russia did eventually intervene in 1827, they took great pains not to antagonise the Sultan;

the commanders of the joint fleets had orders only to maintain a blockade. When they joined battle with Ibrahim's forces in Navarino bay on the west coast of the Peloponnese and defeated them in October 1827, it was officially 'by accident'. Nevertheless, this was the decisive event for the Greek struggle and negotiations began for the establishment of an independent Greek state. The part of Greece which was liberated was only a fraction of Greek-populated lands and there were still many obstacles to be overcome.

Firstly, there was the question of who were to be the Greek leaders. The military leaders who had emerged during the fighting were torn by rivalries amongst themselves and could not easily make the transition from loyalty to their individual communities to a concept of Greece as a single nation. Yet, from their point of view, as expressed by such patriots as General Makriyannis, the professional politicians were self-seekers who showed no appreciation of the sacrifices made by local commanders in the long struggle against the Turks. Inevitably, however, leadership fell to those who had been educated abroad and with whom the European leaders could most easily communicate. For the new state had, at that time, to rely for its existence on the European protecting powers. These powers established a mutually-acceptable monarchy in Greece in 1833 with Prince Otho of Bavaria as its first king. All official positions were initially held by Bavarians and the Greeks had to stage a revolt in 1843 to obtain a formal constitution. This new kingdom of Greece extended only as far as a northern frontier running from from the Gulf of Arta to the Gulf of Volos and included only the islands nearest to the mainland.

A second task during this period was the definition of the official language of the new Greek state. The spoken language of the nineteenth century was insufficient for the needs of a modern state, while the Attic style favoured by the Byzantine administration had fallen out of use. Many educated Greeks, however, spoke a form of the language which was a compromise between demotic and classical Greek and it was such a purified form, advocated by an expatriate Greek scholar, Adamantios Korais, which King Otho's government eventually adopted.

Korais was a Greek from Smyrna who lived in Paris and, although trained as a physician, had devoted his life to the study of the Greek language. He did not intend that the Greeks should return to speaking ancient Greek but he hoped that they would adopt a form of the language which was corrected in such a way as to restore its purity by the elimination of foreign influences which had accumulated within the vernacular speech over the centuries. He restructured the grammar and rejected all

65

loan words, suggesting such compromises as the use of τὸ ὀμμάτιον (eye) instead of τὸ μάτι (demotic) or ὁ ὀφθαλμός (AG), and τὸ ὀψάριον (fish) instead of τὸ ψάρι (demotic) or ὁ ἰχθυς (AG). Both ὀμμάτιον and ὀψάριον, in any case, had their roots in classical Greek. (AG ὄμμα ὄμματος—eye; AG ἕψω—to boil, ὄψον—boiled meat or any delicacy; the chief delicacy of the Athenians was fish.) Schools were founded based on his principles and these produced a generation of educated young men whose use of his form of the language was an added support to its adoption by the new government.

The following example of Korais' katharevousa is taken from his translation of St Paul's Epistle to Titus I. 11.[23]

Τοὺς ὁποίους χρεωστοῦμεν νὰ ἐπιστομίζωμεν. Αὐτοὶ ἀνα- ποδογυρίζουν ὁλοκλήρους οἰκίας, διδάσκοντες, διὰ κέρδος αἰσχρὸν, ὅσα δὲν πρέπει [νὰ διδάσκωνται].

Such men must be curbed because they are ruining whole families by teaching things they should not, and all for sordid gain.[24]

It is interesting to compare Korais' version both with the original text and with a translation published in Geneva in 1638.

Original text:
Οὓς δεῖ ἐπιστομίζειν· οἵτινες ὅλους οἴκους ἀνατρέπουσιν διδάσκοντες ἃ μὴ δεῖ, αἰσχροῦ κέρδους χάριν.

Translation of 1638:
Τοὺς ὁποίους πρέπει νὰ τοὺς ἀποστομώνωμεν· οἱ ὁποῖοι ὀλάκαιρα ὀσπήτια γυρίζουσιν ἄνω κάτω, ἔστωντας νὰ διδάσκουσιν ἐκεῖνα ὁποῦ δὲν πρέπει, διὰ ἄσχημον κέρδος.[23]

The 1638 version has a history worth mentioning. It was made by a monk, Maximus Callipolites, using a form of Greek which would be intelligible to the masses, under the authorisation of the Cretan-born Patriarch of Constantinople, Cyril Loukaris. Loukaris is an interesting figure because of his sympathetic approaches towards Protestantism in his life-long concern to defend Orthodoxy against Jesuit propaganda. Loukaris had the original and 'modern' versions printed in parallel columns but even so the work aroused great anger and was subsequently condemned and burned. (Cyril Loukaris also became a good friend of the English ambassador in

Constantinople at the time, Sir Thomas Roe, and when Sir Thomas returned to England, Loukaris sent as a gift for King Charles I the famous Codex Alexandrinus manuscript of the Bible.)

To return to Korais, however, we should notice that his version is closer to the original than the 1638 version. He chooses οἰκίας rather than ὁσπήτια (Latin derivation—see page 21) but he likes the non-classical ἀναποδογυρίζουν (turn upside down—ἀνὰ πόδι). He uses the classical form of the subjunctive, ἐπιστομίζωμεν, which in everyday language would be ἐπιστομίζομεν (identical pronunciation), and the classical present participle, διδάσκοντες, which, although remaining in use to a limited extent , had come to be popularly expressed by an indeclinable form, e.g. διδάσκοντας.

Korais' purified Greek was attacked by both 'atticisers' and 'demoticists' and there were many attempts to provide alternative versions, but it survived as the official language of Greece up to recent times. Meanwhile the demotic form of the language, based on the spoken κοινή of the Peloponnese, was used alongside it.

For most of the present century the Greek language has had these two major forms, katharevousa (καθαρεύουσα—the purifying language) and demotic (δημοτική—the people's language), terms which, in fact, did not become widely used until towards the end of the nineteenth century. Katharevousa was the official language of the state, the language of scientific and technical writing and, in a slightly modified form, the language of the newspapers. Demotic was the language of everyday speech and of almost all creative writing. In vocabulary, katharevousa generally tried to preserve the consistency of more classical forms of words whereas demotic used the forms that had evolved over the centuries in the spoken language. For example, the word for 'bread' is ἄρτος in katharevousa and ψωμί in demotic. The fact that a baker's shop, however, is an ἀρτοπωλεῖον causes no difficulty. The word for the moon in katharevousa is the same as the ancient Greek word ἡ σελήνη but in demotic it is τὸ φεγγάρι, a diminutive of the classical φέγγος (light).

Katharevousa used a wider range of prepositions and the genitive case continued to be used after certain prepositions. In declensions and conjugations the more classical ending might be used, as in τοὺς ἐπισκέπτας and τῆς πόλεως. A greater variety of prepositional prefixes existed for the formation of compounds and these were particularly useful in technical or official communications. Words such as ἐπανασύνθεσις (reconstruction), αὐτοδιοίκησις (self-government) and διαπραγματεύσεις (negotiations) could not be expressed so precisely in demotic.

On the other hand, demotic had a particularly rich potential for the formation of compounds by juxtaposition, as has already been mentioned, in such words as Σαββατοκύριακο (weekend) and ἀνεβοκαταβαίνω (I go up and down). Creative writers can use this facility to coin an infinite variety of new words such as Kazantzakis' κουφογονάτισε—he became light-kneed (his knees gave way) and ἀργυροτριανταφυλλένιο—silvery-rose coloured. Each form of the language has something to offer and today's Standard Modern Greek, ἡ κοινὴ νεοελληνική, has demotic structure but accepts katharevousa vocabulary where appropriate. This form of the language has now been accepted all over Greece.

The first extract from this period is an example of the demotic language of the beginning of the nineteenth century, taken from the memoirs of **General Makriyannis** (1797–1864). Makriyannis was born of a peasant family near Lidoriki in the mountains of Roumeli and rose to become one of the great commanders of the War. After independence was won, he set himself the task of learning to write in order to put on record his achievements and his beliefs about his country. The memoirs were not published until the beginning of this century when his phonetic spelling was transcribed into a recognisable form. He apologises in his introduction for his lack of learning:

Δὲν ἔπρεπε νὰ ἔμπω εἰς αὐτὸ τὸ ἔργον, ἕνας ἀγράμματος, νὰ βαρύνω τοὺς τίμιους ἀναγνῶστες καὶ μεγάλους ἄντρες καὶ σοφοὺς τῆς κοινωνίας καὶ νὰ τοὺς βάλω σὲ βάρος, νὰ τοὺς κινῶ τὴν περιέργειά τους καὶ νὰ χάνουν τὶς πολυ-τίμητες στιγμὲς εἰς αὐτά. 'Αφοῦ ὅμως ἔλαβα καὶ ἐγὼ ὡς ἄνθρωπος αὐτήνη τὴν ἀδυναμίαν, σᾶς ζητῶ συγνώμη εἰς τὸ βάρος ὁπού θὰ σᾶς δώσω.

An unlettered man like myself should not embark on such a work, to annoy honest readers and the great and learned men of the public and to put them to the annoyance of having their curiosity aroused, only then to waste minutes of their precious time. However, as this lack of skill has fallen to my lot, I ask your pardon for any trouble I put you to.[25]

In fact, his language is very expressive, full of vitality and passion. It differs very little from modern demotic Greek. In the passage below, he reminds his readers of the sufferings of the people of Roumeli at the hands of the Turks and reveals his anger against the leaders of the nation for allowing this effort to go to waste in the civil strife of 1824.

Ἀφοῦ θέλησε ὁ θεὸς νὰ γίνωμε κι' ἐμεῖς ἔθνος, δι' αὐτὸ σκλαβώθηκαν οἱ σημαντικοὶ τῆς Ρούμελης, σκοτώθηκαν, θυσιάστηκαν· ἦταν νοικοκυραῖοι, ἔγιναν διακοναραῖοι· κι' ἄλλοι διὰ τὴν πατρίδα ἔλειψαν καὶ χάθηκαν ὁλότελα. Αὐτοὶ πρὶν ἀπὸ τὴν ἐπανάστασιν βάσταξαν τὴν πατρίδα ὅσο ν' ἄβρη μίαν ἡμέρα ἁρμόδια νὰ λευτερωθῆ καθὼς ὁ Θεὸς φώτισε κι' ἐβρέθη.

...

Πέστε μου ἔνα σπίτι παλιὸν εἰς τὴν Ρούμελη ὁποὺ νὰ μὴν εἶναι χτίριον μοναχά. Πέστε μου πολιτείαν νὰ μὴν κάηκε καὶ οἱ γὲς ἔρημες καὶ μπαίρια ὡς τὴν σήμερον. Σᾶς εἶπα τὶς θυσίες τῆς Ρούμελης. Κι' ἀδικημένη εἶναι κι' ἀφανισμένη. Νόμους γυρεύει καὶ σύστημα νὰ πάγη ἡ πατρὶς ὀμπρός. Ὁ Κολοκοτρώνης ὅμως κι' ὁ Μεταξᾶς καὶ οἱ ἄλλοι οἱ τοιοῦτοι καθημερινοὺς ἐφύλιους πολέμους θέλουν καὶ φατρίες· αὐτῆνοι τὶς γέννησαν κι' ἀπὸ αὐτοὺς προχώρεσαν κι' οἱ Ἀράπηδες.

(Chapter Six—Καημένη Ρούμελη)

Ἀράπηδες—the Egyptians, under Ibrahim Pasha from 1825 onwards.

As it was the will of God that we too should become a nation, for this cause the leading men of Roumeli have suffered slavery, death and every sacrifice. They were men of substance and have become beggars; others have died for their country and are utterly lost. Before the revolution these men maintained their country till the right day should be found for her freedom, as through God's light it was found.

...

Tell me of one ancient house in Roumeli that is now more than its bare walls! Tell me of a city that has not been burnt to the ground and its lands untilled and desolate to this day! I have told you what sacrifices Roumeli has made. And she is wronged and ravaged. Our country needs law and order if it is to go ahead: but Kolokotronis and Metaxas and others of their kind stir up civil war and faction every day: it was they who gave birth to this and it was through them that the Arabs were able to advance.[26]

69

Verbs

Most of the verbs in this passage conform to the standard patterns of modern Greek, apart from a few cases where the more classical form is found as in γίνωμε which retains the ω in the subjunctive and ἐβρέθη for the aorist passive rather than the modern βρέθηκε. The basic verbal scheme of modern Greek, using δένω (to tie) as the paradigm, is as follows:

i) There are three basic stems: the present δεν (δένω), the aorist active δεσ (ἔδεσα) and the aorist passive δεθ (δέθηκα).

ii) The tenses in most frequent use are the present, imperfect, aorist and future. The perfect tenses, formed with the help of ἔχω, are not frequently used, since the aorist can also represent perfect and pluperfect.

iii) Modern Greek distinguishes two kinds of action, one being timeless, either in progress or repeated, the other being a single action complete in itself. The former can be termed the 'imperfective' aspect (ἄτελες) and is formed from the present stem, the latter can be termed the 'perfective' aspect (τέλειο) and is formed from the aorist stems.

iv) The following tables illustrate the main indicative tenses of modern Greek, according to their basic stem.

Present Stem—δεν (imperfective)

	Active	Passive
Present	δένω—I am tying	δένομαι
Imperfect	ἔδενα—I was tying	δενόμουν
Future	θὰ δένω—I shall be tying, I shall tie (repeatedly, from time to time)	θὰ δένομαι

Aorist Active Stem—δεσ (perfective)

Aorist	ἔδεσα—I tied
Future	θὰ δέσω—I shall tie (on a specific occasion)

Aorist Passive Stem—δεθ (perfective)

Aorist	δέθηκα—I was tied
Future	θὰ δεθῶ—I shall be tied

Also formed from the aorist stems are the following perfect tenses:

70

	Active	Passive
Perfect	ἔχω δέσει	ἔχω δεθεῖ
Pluperfect	εἶχα δέσει	εἶχα δεθεῖ
Future Perfect	θὰ ἔχω δέσει	θὰ ἔχω δεθεῖ

The forms δέσει and δεθεῖ are a transformation of the ancient infinitives δέσειν (for δέσαι) and δεθῆναι.

v) The infinitive has disappeared in modern Greek. Its place is usually taken by νὰ and the subjunctive.

vi) The subjunctive and imperative also have two aspects:

Imperfective

	Active	Passive
Subjunctive	νὰ δένω	νὰ δένομαι
Imperative	δένε/δένετε	δένου/δένεστε

Perfective

	Active	Passive
Subjunctive	νὰ δέσω	νὰ δεθῶ
Imperative	δέσε/δέστε	δέσου/δεθεῖτε

In the spoken language the forms of the indicative and subjunctive are usually identical. The subjunctive is mainly found in secondary clauses, most commonly distinguished by νὰ (AG ἵνα) or μὴ but also found with ἂς (ἄφες—leave, allow) e.g. ἂς ἔρθει—let him come.

Vocabulary

Apart from τὸ μπαΐρι—uncultivated area (from the Turkish word bayir), σκλαβώνω and σπίτι, the vocabulary of this passage is wholly Greek in derivation. νοικοκύρης—a householder—comes from the classical οἰκοκύριος. διακονιάρης—a beggar—is formed from διακονία which in ancient Greek means 'service' but which has derived its new meaning from the service of monks who went round houses collecting charity for their monasteries. γυρεύω—to search/look for—is formed from γῦρος which in ancient Greek is a 'ring' or 'circle' and in modern Greek also means 'a circuit' or 'a walk (around)'. ἐφύλιος (ἐμφύλιος) and φατρία (φράτρα) are classical, meaning 'among the people/civil' and 'tribe/political division' respectively. Λευτερώνω is the shortened form of ἐλευθερώνω, λευτερία and ἐλευθερία both being in common use in demotic Greek.

71

This early example of demotic is truly Greek. Greece's language problem was not one of bilingualism but one of two different forms of the same language and yet, unfortunately, it became the source of much passionate dispute for several generations.

Nineteenth century demotic Greek found its earliest literary advocates among the poets of the Ionian Islands. These islands had remained under the rule of Venice and free of the Turkish yoke and they had also inherited the demotic literary tradition of Crete after that island's fall to the Turks in the seventeenth century. In 1797 they were taken over by Napoleon and then they passed under a series of foreign rulers, including the French, the Russians and the Turks. They eventually came into British hands in 1814. A study of the fifty years of British influence in the islands and of the personalities of the Britons who lived there or paid visits would be fascinating but is out of place here. In 1864 the islands were ceded to the kingdom of Greece.

By this time, however, writers of the Ionian Islands had already made a name for themselves. The British had founded a university on Corfu, the Ionian Academy, which had encouraged the study of Greek. Although the upper classes had been very much influenced by Venetian culture, Greek poetry had always been loved and in the nineteenth century it received an impetus from the publication of the Δημοτικὰ Τραγούδια. Poets such as Dionysius Solomos, Aristotelis Valaoritis and Andreas Kalvos were to give this poetry a literary form.

Dionysius Solomos (1798–1857) had begun writing in Italian but soon changed to Greek and took up the demotic tradition with its themes of freedom, death and nature. The first verses of his 'Ode to Liberty', quoted below, became the Greek National Anthem.

Σὲ γνωρίζω ἀπὸ τὴν κόψη
τοῦ σπαθιοῦ τὴν τρομερή,
σὲ γνωρίζω ἀπὸ τὴν ὄψη
ποὺ μὲ βία μετράει τὴ γῆ.

'Απ' τὰ κόκαλα βγαλμένη
τῶν Ἑλλήνων τὰ ἱερά,
καὶ σὰν πρῶτα ἀνδρειωμένη
χαῖρε, ὦ χαῖρε, Ἐλευθεριά!

Ἐκεῖ μέσα ἐκατοικοῦσες
πικραμένη, ἐντροπαλή,
κι ἕνα στόμα ἐκαρτεροῦσες,
"ἔλα πάλι ", νά σοῦ πῆ.

Ἄργιε νά 'λθη ἐκείνη ἡ μέρα,
καὶ ἦταν ὅλα σιωπηλά,
γιατὶ τά 'σκιαζε ἡ φοβέρα,
καὶ τὰ πλάκωνε ἡ σκλαβιά.

By the length of thy stride,
By the sweep of thy blade,
By thy countenance stern,
I know thee, proud maid.

The bones of the Hellenes
Have hallowed the tale.
As of old thou art standing:
Hail, Liberty, hail!

Withdrawn into darkness,
Shy, bitter, in pain,
The call wast thou waiting
To come forth again.

Long, long wast thou waiting,
Late, late came the call:
In the tomb of oppression
Fear held us in thrall.[27]

Verbs

One further feature of the verbal system in modern Greek is seen here in ἐκατοικοῦσες and ἐκαρτεροῦσες. These are the imperfect tenses of the contracted verbs κατοικῶ (εω) and καρτερῶ (έω). There are two classes of contracted verbs in modern Greek. In one, the present tense ends in –ῶ –ᾶς –ᾱ; in the other, it ends in –ῶ –εῖς –εῖ. In fact, both classes frequently merge. They differ from uncontracted verbs only in the present and imperfect tenses which are set out below using the paradigms ἀγαπῶ (άω)—to love— and θεωρῶ (–έω)—to regard.

Present Tense

Active		Passive	
ἀγαπ ῶ	θεωρ ῶ	ἀγαπι έμαι	θεωρ οῦμαι
ᾱς	εῖς	έσαι	εῖσαι
ᾱ(άει)	εῖ	έται	εῖται
οῦμε (ᾱμε)	οῦμε	όμαστε	ούμαστε
ᾱτε	εῖτε	έστε	εῖστε
οῦν (ᾱνε)	οῦν	οῦνται	οῦνται

Imperfect Tense

Active	Passive
ἀγαποῦσ α	ἀγαπιό μουν
θεωροῦσ ες	θεωρού σουν
ε	νταν
αμε	μαστε
ατε	σαστε
αν	νταν

Both classes correspond to the ancient Greek verbs in –αω and –εω. The ancient Greek –όω verbs have mainly been converted into verbs in –ώνω, e.g.

MG σκοτώνω (to kill) < AG σκοτόω (to darken, blind)

MG διορθώνω (to correct) < AG διορθόω (to make straight)

Other –ώνω verbs in modern Greek, however, are converted from ancient Greek –νυμι verbs, e.g.

MG χώνω (to thrust, bury, hide) < AG χώννυμι (to throw, heap up, bury)

MG στρώνω (to spread, lay) < AG στρώννυμι

MG ὀμώνω (to swear) < AG ὄμνυμι

Vocabulary

i) τρομερός which in ancient Greek means 'trembling' or 'quivering' has the sense of 'frightful' or 'terrible' in modern Greek.

ii) καρτερῶ has the meaning of 'to be patient' in both ancient and modern Greek but in modern Greek it also means 'to wait for'. The word καρτέρι is thus used for an ambush.

iii) ἄργιε = ἀργά—slowly, late. It is derived from the ancient Greek ἀργός (ἀ/εργός)—not working, idle.

iv) πλακώνω means to flatten or press down. This is derived from the ancient Greek noun πλάκα which was anything flat and broad. In modern Greek πλάκα is a slab, paving-stone, slate etc.

v) ἐντροπαλός—shy—is derived from the ancient Greek noun ἐντρο-πή—shame, reproach. In modern Greek the unstressed initial vowel ε is usually dropped, giving ντροπή—shyness, shame.

vi) γιατί is derived from the ancient Greek διὰ τί. In its interrogative use it means 'why' and in its causal use 'because'.

Solomos' greatest work was his *Free Besieged* (Οἱ Ἐλεύθεροι Πο-λιορκημένοι) which remained unfinished at his death. Solomos worked on this poem over a period of twenty years and the surviving extracts were organised into three different versions by Polylas. The poem tells of the last moments of the siege of Mesolonghi by the Turks in the spring of 1826. Although facing certain death, the people of Mesolonghi refused to surrender and asserted their freedom in one final sortie into the midst of the besiegers. In the extract below Solomos reflects on the beauties of nature whose temptations add poignancy to the self-sacrifice about to be made.

Ὁ ᾿Απρίλης μὲ τὸν ῎Ερωτα χορεύουν καὶ γελοῦνε,
κι ὅσ᾿ ἄνθια βγαίνουν καὶ καρποὶ τόσ᾿ ἄρματα σὲ κλειοῦνε.

Λευκὸ βουνάκι πρόβατα κινούμενο βελάζει,
καὶ μὲς στὴ θάλασσα βαθιὰ ξαναπετιέται πάλι,
κι ὁλόλευκο ἐσύσμιξε μὲ τ᾿ οὐρανοῦ τὰ κάλλη.
Καὶ μὲς στῆς λίμνης τὰ νερά, ὅπ᾿ ἔφθασε μ᾿ ἀσπούδα,
ἔπαιξε μὲ τὸν ἴσκιο της γαλάζια πεταλούδα,
ποὺ εὐώδιασε τὸν ὕπνο της μέσα στὸν ἄγριο κρίνο·
τὸ σκουληκάκι βρίσκεται σ᾿ ὥρα γλυκιὰ κι ἐκεῖνο.
Μάγεμα ἡ φύσις κι ὄνειρο στὴν ὀμορφιὰ καὶ χάρη,
ἡ μαύρη πέτρα ὁλόχρυση καὶ τὸ ξερὸ χορτάρι.
Μὲ χίλιες βρύσες χύνεται, μὲ χίλιες γλῶσσες κραίνει·
ὅποιος πεθάνη σήμερα χίλιες φορὲς πεθαίνει.

Τρέμ᾿ ἡ ψυχὴ καὶ ξαστοχᾶ γλυκὰ τὸν ἑαυτό της.
(Σχεδίασμα Δεύτερο 2)

April and Love are dancing and laughing, but while the trees blossom and bear fruit, so the weapons are closing in.

A massed flock of white sheep moves and bleats. The vision plunges deep in the sea but re-emerges whiter than ever to mingle with the beauty of the sky.

And a blue butterfly, having enjoyed sweet slumber in a wild lily, came hurrying to the waters of the lake and played there with its shadow.

Even the worm enjoyed that happy hour.

Nature is like a spell; her beauty and grace a dream. The black stone and the dry grass are pure gold.

A thousand springs gush forth and a thousand voices cry: 'He who dies today, a thousand deaths will die.'

The soul trembles and, in all its sweetness, forgets itself.

The language is lyrical and full of colour. Diminutives are deliberately used as in βουνάκι and σκουληκάκι. Σκουλήκι (σκωλήκιον) is itself a diminutive of the ancient Greek σκώληξ, a worm. χορτάρι (χορτάριον), grass, is the diminutive of χόρτος, grass, hay.

Emphasis on light and brightness is given by the adjectives ὁλόλευκο and ὁλόχρυση. The modern Greek prefix ὁλο-, which is frequently used to denote 'all' or 'completely', is also an ancient Greek prefix.

MG   ὁλόκληρος—whole, entire
ὁλότελα—completely
ὁλομόναχος—all alone

AG   ὁλόκληρος—complete in all parts, entire
ὁλοτελής—quite complete, perfect
ὁλόκαυτος—burnt whole

The following forms and derivations are also of interest:

i) ἄνθια, blossoms, is the plural of τὸ ἄνθος. The –ια ending is quite frequently found in literature, although only the regular –η ending is in use today for this type of neuter noun.

ii) ἴσκιος, shadow, is derived from the ancient Greek σκιά and ὀμορφιά, beauty, from the ancient Greek εὐμορφία.

iii) πεθαίνω is the modern Greek verb 'to die' and is derived as follows:
πεθαίνω < ἀπεθαίνω < ἀπέθανον, aorist of AG ἀποθνήσκω.

iv) χύνω, to pour, is also formed from an aorist stem:
χύνω < ἐχύθην, aorist passive of AG χέω.

The novel entered the literary life of the new state later than poetry, largely by way of translations of European works. Among the early Greek prose writers several wrote in katharevousa, the most well-known of these being **Alexander Papadiamantis** (1851–1911) from the island of Skiathos. He was a popular writer in his day and his stories were serialised in the newspapers. People respected him for his sincere dedication to the traditions of Greek religion and the form of his katharevousa was influenced by the language of the Church. The short extract below is from a long historical novel called *The Gipsy Girl*.

Τὸ φέγγος τῆς σελήνης κατήρχετο διὰ τοῦ ἀνοίγματος τῶν δένδρων ἐπὶ τοῦ προσώπου τοῦ ἀγνώστου καὶ ἐφώτισε τοὺς χαρακτῆρας του. Ἦτο ἄνθρωπος μὲ χρῶμα ἡλιοκαὲς ἢ φύσει μελαψόν, μὲ ὀστεώδεις καὶ μακρὰς ἐξοχὰς ἐν τῇ μορφῇ, μὲ ἐρρυτιδωμένον μέτωπον. Ὑψηλὸς τὸ ἀνάστημα, ἀλλὰ κυρτός. Ἐφόρει πενιχρότατα ἐνδύματα. Ἐκ τῶν χειρίδων του ἐξήρχοντο δύο σκελετώδεις βραχίονες, αἱ χεῖρες του δὲ ἦσαν τόσον ρικναὶ καὶ κατάξηροι καὶ μαῦραι, ὥστε ἐφαίνετο ἔχουσαι συγγένειάν τινα μὲ τὰ σκληρὰ μέταλλα, τὸν σίδηρον καὶ τὸν χαλκόν. Ἦτο ἴσως Αἰγύπτιος, ἐξ ἐκείνων οἵτινες μόνοι κατειργάζοντο κατὰ τὸν χρόνον ἐκεῖνον ἐν τῇ Ἀνατολῇ τὰ εἰρημένα μέταλλα.

from Ἡ Γυφτοπούλα

The light of the moon shone down through the opening in the trees on to the face of the stranger and illuminated his features. He was a man of dark complexion, sun-tanned or naturally swarthy, with limbs that looked bony and long and a wrinkled forehead. He was tall in stature but bent and he was wearing very shabby clothes. Out of his sleeves there projected two skeletal-like arms and his hands were wrinkled, dry and black, indicating that his work involved him in the handling of hard metals, such as iron and bronze. Perhaps he was an Egyptian, one of those who at that time used to work these metals in the Middle East.

The pure form of language used here seems well suited to the descriptive nature of the passage. For dialogue Papadiamantis would use a language that was closer to that spoken by the people. Most of the vocabulary is consistent with classical Greek, as in ἡ σελήνη— moon, ἡλιοκαής— sun-burnt, ἡ χειρίς—sleeve and ὁ βραχίων—arm. Demotic Greek equivalents of these would be τὸ φεγγάρι, ἡλιοκαμένος, μανίκι (Latin derivation—'manicae' from 'manus'—hand) and χέρι or μπράτσο (Venetian 'brazzo' < Latin 'bracchium' < AG βραχίων; a full circle!)

The suffixes –μα (forming an abstract noun from a verb) and –ωδες (forming an adjective meaning 'like...') are also used in demotic; their origin is from the late classical language. Examples here are τὸ ἄνοιγμα—opening, τὸ ἀνάστημα—stature, τὸ ἔνδυμα—dress, attire, ὀστεώδης—bony and σκελετώδης—skeletal, like a skeleton.

Two words which have their own intrinsic interest are ἐξοχάς (ἐξοχή) and μέταλλον. Papadiamantis seems to use the former in the sense of 'limbs' or 'hands and feet'. The word literally means 'a protrusion' or 'prominence'. Κατ' ἐξοχὴν is used today in the sense of 'pre-eminently' and it also had this sense in late classical times but the most common meaning of ἡ ἐξοχή today is that of 'countryside'. The interesting feature of μέταλλον is its original derivation. The meaning of the word in ancient Greek is 'mine' or 'quarry' rather than 'metal' and its basic meaning is 'the place of searching' from μετ' ἄλλα—in quest of other things.

By the end of the nineteenth century novelists were turning towards the use of the demotic form of the language for their writing. The leading exponent of the use of demotic in prose was **Ioannis Psicharis** (1854–1929). He was an expatriate Greek who lived in Paris, teaching modern Greek at the Ecole de Langues Orientales and lecturing on philological topics. His basic belief was that languages change and any attempt to reverse the natural course of such development will result in failure. He did not reject ancient Greek but he believed that children should be taught in demotic while also making a proper but separate study of the ancient language. In his own writings he set out to use only the spoken language. He only knew this at second hand, however, as he had never lived in Greece. He may have taken his ideas to extremes, but there can be no doubt that he provided an impetus to other aspiring writers for whom demotic seemed the natural medium where their subject matter was about everyday life and contemporary people. One such writer was Andreas Karkavitsas (1865–1922). He turned to demotic in mid-career and his most famous novel, Ὁ Ζητιάνος—*The Beggar*, makes full use of the spoken language in describing the beggars of Kravara and the wretched life of villagers in Thessaly. Ioannis Kondylakis (1861–1920) also wrote his earlier novels (such as *Patouchas*) in katharevousa but a later one in demotic (*First Love*).

Amongst Psicharis' many writings one novel in particular was intended to be a forthright demonstration of his ideas. Τὸ Ταξίδι Μου was a revelation; its language was demotic Greek without compromise. Its subject matter was a description of a journey Psicharis made in 1886 from Paris to Constantinople and Athens. It is a mixture of narrative, anecdote and satire but it also shows his linguistic ideas in action.

He comments on the use of οἰκία rather than σπίτι as follows:

τὰ σπίτια στὴν ᾿Αθῆνα εἶναι ὡραῖα... Τὸ κακὸ εἶναι ὅμως
ποὺ τὸ σπίτι τὸ λέν' 'οἰκία' καὶ 'οἶκος'.   (Chapter 24)

The houses in Athens are beautiful... The trouble is that they call the
house οἰκία and οἶκος.

N.B. In the rest of this passage he argues that the person who hears the
word οἰκία immediately translates it back to σπίτι in his own mind and
so the mental effort of conversation is doubled.

Elsewhere he writes:

Τὸ ἔθνος λέει ψωμί, νερό, κρασί, κεφάλι, χέρια, ποδάρια.
Εἶναι μάλιστα πανελλήνια. Κι' αὐτὰ γράφουμε.

The people say ψωμί, νερό... These are indeed panhellenic words and
these are the words we write.

(The katharevousa equivalents would be ἄρτος, ὕδωρ, οἶνος, κεφαλή,
χείρ and πούς.)

One of his suggested reforms which has recently been adopted in Greece
is the adaptation of third declension nouns with the form ἡ θέσις τῆς
θέσεως to a first declension form ἡ θέση τῆς θέσης (see page 52).

He also had ideas for changes in spelling. As the pronunciation of αυ
and ευ involved the sounds 'v' and 'f', he suggested the following type of
change: αὔριο to become ἄβριο, Εὐρώπη to become ᾿Εβρώπη and
εὐτυχία to become ἐφτυχία. Other adaptations of his spelling to modern
pronunciation, or what he thought a modern pronunciation should be,
include Γιούλιο for ᾿Ιούλιο, ξήμισυ for ἐξήμισυ, σκέδιο for σχέδιο,
σιδερόδρομο for σιδηρόδρομο and φημερίδα for ἐφημερίδα. These
ideas have not been adopted but a start has now been made to simplify accentuation and to omit breathings. The new monotonic system is taught in
schools and used widely in the press.

At the beginning of the twentieth century **Alexander Pallis**, a busi-
nessman, who believed that the written language should conform to that
generally spoken, wrote a translation of the *Iliad* in demotic. The first
three lines are quoted below, preceded by the Homeric original.

Homer
Μῆνιν ἄειδε, θεά, Πηληϊάδεω 'Αχιλῆος
οὐλομένην, ἣ μυρι' 'Αχαιοῖς ἄλγε' ἔθηκε,
πολλὰς δ' ἰφθίμους ψυχὰς "Αϊδι προΐαψεν
ἡρώων.

Sing, goddess, of the fatal anger of Achilles, Peleus' son, which brought to the Achaeans countless sufferings and sent many stout souls of heroes down to Hades before their time.

Pallis
Τραγούδα, μοῦσα, τὸ θυμὸ τοῦ ξακουστοῦ 'Αχιλλέα,
τὸν ἔρμο, π' ὅλους πότισε τοὺς 'Αχαιοὺς φαρμάκια
καὶ πλῆθος ἔστειλε ψυχὲς λεβέντικες στὸν "Αδη.

Pallis has used the fifteen-syllable line of the popular ballads. He has used ξακουστοῦ (famous) in place of the awkward Πηληϊάδεω and his choice of λεβέντικες for 'heroes' produces a thoroughly modern term, meaning 'fine young men'.

This translation was a revolutionary move but it did not provoke the outcry which was to follow his translation of the Gospels into demotic in 1901. The first few verses of his 'Gospel according to St John', which follow, show how simple his style was and yet the publication was the occasion of riots in the streets of Athens, so strongly revered was the official language and the standing of the Church.

St John I. 1–6
Στὴν ἀρχὴ εἶταν ὁ λόγος κι' ὁ λόγος εἴτανε μὲ τὸ Θεὸ καὶ Θεὸς εἶταν ὁ λόγος. Εἶταν ἐκεῖνος στὴν ἀρχὴ μὲ τὸ Θεό. Ὅλα τὰ πάντα μέσω τοῦ ἔγιναν, καὶ χωρὶς του τίποτα δὲν ἔγινε ποὺ γίνηκε. Μέσα τοῦ εἴτανε ζωὴ κι' ἡ ζωὴ εἴτανε τὸ φῶς τῶν ἀνθρώπων, καὶ τὸ φῶς μέσα στὸ σκοτάδι φέγγει καὶ τὸ σκοτάδι δὲν τὸ κυρίεψε.

(Compare this with the original: Ἐν ἀρχῇ ἦν ὁ λόγος, καὶ ὁ λόγος ἦν πρὸς τὸν θεόν, καὶ θεὸς ἦν ὁ λόγος. οὗτος ἦν ἐν ἀρχῇ πρὸς τὸν θεόν. πάντα δι' αὐτοῦ ἐγένετο, καὶ χωρὶς αὐτοῦ ἐγένετο οὐδὲ ἕν. ὃ γέγονεν ἐν αὐτῷ ζωὴ ἦν, καὶ ἡ ζωὴ ἦν τὸ φῶς τῶν ἀνθρώπων· καὶ τὸ φῶς ἐν τῇ σκοτίᾳ φαίνει, καὶ ἡ σκοτία αὐτὸ οὐ κατέλαβεν.)

It is not possible in a book such as this to attempt to analyse the reasons for the controversy which surrounded katharevousa and demotic at the beginning of the twentieth century. During the second half of the nineteenth century katharevousa had been progressively purified and had moved further apart from the vernacular. There was bitter hostility towards the radical demoticists who were given the nickname μαλλιαροί (long-haired). Nevertheless, the demotic language continued to develop as a literary medium, some writers taking it to extremes and others combining considerable katharevousa elements with demotic in their prose or poetry. The selection of twentieth-century writings in the next chapter will perhaps give some idea of this variety of styles.

In 1907 Kazantzakis produced a manifesto on behalf of demotic and in 1917 the government of his fellow-Cretan, Venizelos, introduced demotic into the elementary schools for the first time.

The 'language question' was most keenly felt in education and government instructions would change almost from year to year as to whether demotic should be taught at all levels or only for the first three years or not at all. For example, in the period between 1933 and 1937 all textbooks written in demotic were recalled. In 1941 demotic was reintroduced with a new Grammar written by Manos Triantaphyllidis. This was the first formal definition of demotic grammar. Between 1967 and 1974, under the military dictatorship, katharevousa was used but in 1976 Constantine Karamanlis' government decided that the teaching at all levels of education should be solely in demotic. A new edition of Triantaphyllidis' Grammar was brought out with some alterations and considerable improvements in presentation. Today this is not only the obligatory school textbook but it is also used by all branches of the Civil Service . The move towards a standard demotic in the establishment of Standard Modern Greek has been generally welcomed, although certain sections of the universities have argued for the production of an entirely new school Grammar in which there should be more emphasis on the basic concepts of the language. This is seen to be particularly important now that ancient Greek is no longer compulsory in schools. Outside Greece an interest in the study of the modern Greek language seems to be growing and it is to be hoped that the literature of modern Greece may also become available to a wider readership. The final chapter will give a selection of some of the writings of the present century. For those seeking a more detailed analysis, I recommend the works of literary criticism referred to in the bibliography.

CHAPTER FIVE

THE TWENTIETH CENTURY: A SELECTION

The twentieth century has seen progress for Greece in the face of a succession of disasters. The early years of the century were characterised by a desire to extend the frontiers to include lands with a sizeable Greek population which were historically Greek. Following a decade of struggles in Macedonia, principally between Greek and Bulgarian armed bands, the main rival groups eventually agreed on a Balkan alliance to oppose Turkey. This led to the wars of 1912–13 which resulted in the doubling of Greek territory and population to include Northern Greece, Crete and the eastern Aegean islands excluding the Dodecanese. At this time, too, Greece acquired a strong leader in the person of Eleutherios Venizelos from Crete. This hopeful start to the century, however, was followed by serious internal problems during the First World War when the country was split between supporters of the king who believed that the country could remain neutral and the followers of Venizelos, his prime minister, who offered to help the Allies.

The few years following the war were to awaken hopes of a further recovery of territory and this was with the active encouragement of the Allies who invited the Greeks to occupy the Smyrna district of Asia Minor on behalf of the League of Nations. These hopes were short-lived, however. In 1922 a military disaster in Asia Minor was followed by the descent of the Turks to the coast and the destruction of Smyrna. About 12,000 Greeks were murdered or died in the flames of the burning city. Those who could leave, mainly women and children, fled by sea but many of the men were forcibly taken into the interior to form labour battalions. In this situation Greece found herself alone. Winston Churchill called it a true Greek tragedy and its effects were felt for many generations to come.

The catastrophe was followed by the Treaty of Lausanne with its agreement on a population exchange between Greece and Turkey. This was an exchange on a massive scale and it resulted in one-and-a-half million destitute Greek refugees having to be settled in an already poor country of five million. The critical situation created by this influx of people and the unstable political conditions of the time led to a decade of intense economic difficulty and personal suffering. Nevertheless, the refugees were absorbed and housed, a tremendous achievement, and gradually a positive side to the situation began to emerge. In addition to being hard-working and inventive, the newcomers had brought with them useful skills in agriculture and considerable experience of business. Constantinople and Smyrna had been important commercial centres and their businessmen had a cosmopolitan outlook which was a great asset to their new environment.

If all had gone smoothly, the decade of the forties should have seen the emergence of a confident nation but, instead, the country was plunged into fresh troubles. War with Italy in 1940 was followed by the German occupation of 1941 to 1944 which was accompanied by widespread starvation and terror. Then there followed a series of civil wars, so that fighting in Greece did not end until 1949. During ten years of conflict there had been a million casualties which was ten per cent of the population.

It was only after 1950 that reconstruction was able to proceed without serious interruption but Greece had a long way to go to achieve widespread prosperity and the kind of political stability taken for granted in other European countries. Increasing political chaos in the mid 1960s led to a coup d'etat by a group of army officers in 1967. The military regime lasted for seven years until an Athens-backed coup in Cyprus followed by the Turkish invasion of that island brought about its downfall in 1974 and led to the recall of Constantine Karamanlis to form a government. In the meantime, the royal family had fled after an early attempted counter-coup. They were never to return and the abolition of the monarchy was confirmed by a plebiscite held under Karamanlis' government at the end of 1974.

The new Republic was gradually able to make much-needed political and social reforms and in 1980 was admitted as a member of the EEC. Conservatism under Constantine Karamanlis was succeeded by socialism under Andreas Papandreou. Ties with the West will be strengthened with the opening up of the European Community in 1992 and talks with Turkey proceed in anticipation of that country too becoming a member state. These achievements should not be underestimated. Anyone who wishes to know Greece and the Greeks must understand their history.

Of the writers whose extracts follow, Costis Palamas bridged the centuries and wrote during a period of optimism. Constantine Cavafy was outside the mainstream of political events, living in Alexandria, but Ilias Venezis was very much within it; he and his family were victims of the Asia Minor catastrophe. Nikos Kazantzakis was a troubled spirit of the middle decades who only turned to writing novels in his later years whereas Pantelis Prevelakis, his fellow-Cretan and friend, has written novels throughout his life, most of which are devoted to Cretan themes. George Seferis and Odysseus Elytis were both awarded Nobel Prizes for Literature for their poetry, Seferis in 1963 and Elytis in 1979. The new spirit which they introduced to poetry was an important influence in the second half of the century. Antonis Samarakis represents a trend in prose writing which has many representatives, a preoccupation with the life of the city and man's struggle to come to terms with the political and social issues he meets there.[28]

Costis Palamas (1859–1943)

Palamas was born in Patras in 1859 and was educated in Mesolonghi but he spent most of his life in Athens. He was an establishment figure in that he had been appointed secretary of the University of Athens in 1897 but at the same time he was anti-establishment in his literary activities. After an attempt to write in katharevousa he had settled on demotic as the best medium for his poetry.

In the 'Dodecalogue of the Gipsy' Palamas traces a gipsy poet's attempt to come to terms with himself. In his own introduction to the poem Palamas identifies himself with this gipsy; he admires the gipsy's freedom and sympathises with his feeling of alienation from the other gipsies. The gipsy finally finds release in a violin just as Palamas does in his poetry. The poem is not historical but there is one specific event in it when the gipsy people gather in Thrace a hundred years before the fall of Constantinople. In the following extract the gipsy poet is riding his mule alone and reflecting on the life of his fellow-gipsies from whom he stands apart.

Οὔτε σπίτια, οὔτε καλύβια
δὲ σοῦ πόδισαν ποτέ,
δὲ σοῦ κάρφωσαν τὸ δρόμο
τὸν παντοτινό, τὸν ἀνεμπόδιστο,
Γύφτε, ἀταίριαστε λαέ.
Τῆς στεριᾶς τὰ τρεχαντήρια,
νὰ τἀδάμαστα μουλάρια!
Τἄρμενά τους εἶναι τὰ τσαντήρια·

84

νὰ παλάτια, ἰδὲς ναοί!
Σ' ἕνα παίξιμο ματιῶν ἐδῶ καὶ ἐκεῖ
χτίζονται καὶ ὑψώνονται καὶ πᾶνε
καὶ γκρεμίζονται, ὅπως πᾶνε,
ὕστερ' ἀπ' τὸ χτίσμα κι ἀπ' τὸν ὑψωμό,
ὅσα πλάθει ὁ λογισμός μας κάτου ἐδῶ.
Καὶ δὲν εἶναι ὁ γύφτος τοῦ σπιτιοῦ ραγιᾶς,
καὶ τὸ σπίτι ἔχει φτερούγια σὰν ἐμᾶς,
καὶ τὸ σπίτι ἀκολουθάει,
καὶ εἶν' αὐτὸ πιστὸ
στὸν εἶν' αὐτὸ πιστὸ
στὸν ἀφέντη, ὄχι ἐκεῖνος πρὸς αὐτό...
Κι ἐγὼ λέω σὲ σᾶς ἀνάμεσα,
στοὺς ξεχωριστοὺς ξεχωριστός·
Οὔτε σπίτια, οὔτε καλύβια, οὔτε τσαντήρια·
στὸ μεγάλο ἀφεντοπάλατο τῆς πλάσης
μιὰ μονάκριβη σκεπή μου· ὁ οὐρανός!
...
...
...

Κι ἐγὼ μέσα στὸ τρικύμισμα
καὶ στὴ χαλαοὴ τοῦ κόσμου
κάτι γνώριζα ποὺ ἀρπάζοντας
μὲ ξεχώριζε καὶ μὲ εἶχεν
ἀποπάνω ἀπ' τὸ τρικύμισμα
κι ἀπ' τὴ χαλαοὴ τοῦ κόσμου·
δούλεμα δὲν εἴτανε φτεροῦ,
καὶ χεριοῦ δὲν εἶταν ἀνασήκωμα,
καὶ δὲν εἶταν πύργος ἢ κορφή·
ἄλλη σκάλα κι ἄλλο ἀνέβασμα,
καὶ εἴτανε τὰ ὕψη ἀλλοῦ·
καὶ εἴτανε σὰν ἀξεδιάλυτο
ὕπνου ἀξύπνητου χρυσόνειρο,
ποὺ ποτὲ δὲν πάτησε στὴ γῆ,
πόχει ἀλλοῦ, ἀπὸ πέρα, τὴν πηγή,
καὶ ποὺ ἀπλώνεται ἀνεβαίνοντας
ὅλο πέρα καὶ ὅλο πέρα,
ὣς ποὺ νέο στοιχεῖο γίνεται,
κάτι σὰν αἰθέρας τοῦ αἰθέρα.

Κι ἔτσι στὰ πανάλαφρα,
στὰ πανύψηλα ἔτσι ἐγὼ εἴμουν
μέσα στοὺς ξεχωριστοὺς
ὁ ξεχωριστὸς ἐγὼ εἴμουν,
ὅλα μέσα μου τὰ νιάτα
κι ὅλα τὰ γεράματα
καὶ τοὺς σπόρους καὶ τὶς μῆτρες
κλειῶντας ἀξεχώριστα!

Ο Δωδεκάλογος τοῦ Γύφτου
from Λόγος Πρῶτος, Ο Ερχομός

Gipsy people, peerless and apart,
No house or hut ever halted your age-old pilgrimage.
Look at your sloops, the tireless mules, their sails the tents!
Look at your palaces, your temples!
Here and there, at a glance of the eye, they spring up,
Then they go and are all ruined as they go,
All that our thought fashions here below.
The Gipsy is no house-slave.
His house is bound to him, not he to house.
And I, one set apart among a people set apart, I say to you:
No house, no hut, no tent!
Mine is the palace of the lord of creation, my only roof the sky.
...
...
In the turmoil of the world I have known something
That has set me apart and raised me above it,
No stroke of a wing, no thrust of a hand,
No tower, no hilltop, no, by another ascent, another stair,
I have climbed to other heights, buoyed up
By a vision never earth-bound that rises and expands
Into another element, more ethereal than the ether,
And so in the loftiest zone I live alone,
One set apart among a people set apart,
With youth and age, seed and womb enclosed inseparably within me.

Translated by George Thomson[29]

Constantine Cavafy (1863–1932)

The other great national Greek poet of the early twentieth century was Cavafy, but his background was quite different. He lived in the cosmopolitan atmosphere of Alexandria, a city with memories of an illustrious Hellenistic past. This was the background which Cavafy chose for his poetry but whether set in the past or the present, the human dilemmas and the human emotions which he depicts are timeless. The poems are generally short and the language is a unique mixture of his own. Peter Bien quotes one of Cavafy's own remarks on this. 'Of course we should write in demotic. But...the artisan of words has the duty to combine what is beautiful with what is alive.'[30]

The two poems given here are rich in patterning of rhyme and words. In 'The City' Cavafy is reflecting on the impossibility of escaping from aspects of one's own personality. 'Ithaka' has a more positive message. It is life itself which we should value; the quality of life is what the individual makes of it.

Ἡ Πόλις

Εἶπες· "Θὰ πάγω σ' ἄλλη γῆ, θὰ πάγω σ' ἄλλη θάλασσα.
Μιὰ πόλις ἄλλη θὰ βρεθεῖ καλλίτερη ἀπὸ αὐτή.
Κάθε προσπάθεια μου μιὰ καταδίκη εἶναι γραφτή·
κ' εἶν' ἡ καρδιά μου—σὰν νεκρὸς—θαμένη.
Ὁ νοῦς μου ὡς πότε μὲς στὸν μαρασμὸν αὐτὸν θὰ μένει;
Ὅπου τὸ μάτι μου γυρίσω, ὅπου κι ἂν δῶ
ἐρείπια μαῦρα τῆς ζωῆς μου βλέπω ἐδῶ,
ποὺ τόσα χρόνια πέρασα καὶ ρήμαξα καὶ χάλασα ".

Καινούριους τόπους δὲν θὰ βρεῖς, δὲν θἄβρεις ἄλλες
                                              θάλασσες.
Ἡ πόλις θὰ σὲ ἀκολουθεῖ. Στοὺς δρόμους θὰ γυρνᾶς
τοὺς ἴδιους. Καὶ στὲς γειτονιὲς τὲς ἴδιες θὰ γερνᾶς·
καὶ μὲς στὰ ἴδια σπίτια αὐτὰ θ' ἀσπρίζεις.
Πάντα στὴν πόλι αὐτὴ θὰ φθάνεις. Γιὰ τὰ ἀλλοῦ—μὴ
                                              ἐλπίζεις—
δὲν ἔχει πλοῖο γιὰ σέ, δὲν ἔχει ὁδο.
Ἔτσι ποὺ τὴ ζωή σου ρήμαξες ἐδῶ
στὴν κώχη τούτη τὴν μικρή, σ' ὅλην τὴν γῆ τὴν χάλασες.

The City
You said: 'I'll go to another land, go to another sea,
find some other town better than this one.
Fated, condemned, is all that I've ever done

87

and my heart, like a dead body, is buried in a tomb.
How long must my mind remain within this gloom?
When I cast my eyes about me, look no matter where,
I see the black ruins of my life, here,
where I've spent so many years—wasted them, destroyed them
utterly.'

You will not find new lands, not find another sea.
The city will follow you. You'll wander down
these very streets, age in these same quarters of the town,
among the same houses finally turn grey.
You'll reach this city always. Don't hope to get away:
for you there is no ship, no road anywhere.
As you've destroyed your life here,
in this small corner, so in the whole world you've wrecked it
utterly.
Translated by Rae Dalvern[31]

Ἰθάκη

Σὰ βγεῖς στὸν πηγαιμὸ γιὰ τὴν Ἰθάκη,
νὰ εὔχεσαι νἆναι μακρὺς ὁ δρόμος,
γεμάτος περιπέτειες, γεμάτος γνώσεις.
Τοὺς Λαιστρυγόνας καὶ τοὺς Κύκλωπας,
τὸν θυμωμένο Ποσειδῶνα μὴ φοβᾶσαι,
τέτοια στὸν δρόμο σου ποτέ σου δὲν θὰ βρεῖς,
ἂν μέν' ἡ σκέψις σου ὑψηλή, ἂν ἐκλεκτὴ
συγκίνησις τὸ πνεῦμα καὶ τὸ σῶμα σου ἀγγιζει.
Τοὺς Λαιστρυγόνας καὶ τοὺς Κύκλωπας,
τὸν ἄγριο Ποσειδῶνα δὲν θὰ συναντήσεις,
ἂν δὲν τοὺς κουβανεῖς μὲς στὴν ψυχή σου,
ἂν ἡ ψυχή σου δὲν τοὺς στήνει ἐμπρός σου.

Νὰ εὔχεσαι νἆναι μακρὺς ὁ δρόμος.
Πολλὰ τὰ καλοκαιρινὰ πρωϊὰ νὰ εἶναι
ποὺ μὲ τί εὐχαρίστησι, μὲ τί χαρὰ
θὰ μπαίνεις σὲ λιμένας πρωτοειδωμένους·
νὰ σταματήσεις σ' ἐμπορεῖα Φοινικικά,
καὶ τὲς καλὲς πραγμάτειες ν' ἀποκτήσεις,
σεντέφια καὶ κοράλλια, κεχριμπάρια κ' ἔβενους,
καὶ ἡδονικὰ μυρωδικὰ κάθε λογῆς,

ὅσο μπορεῖς πιὸ ἄφθονα ἡδονικὰ μυρωδικά·
σὲ πόλεις Αἰγυπτιακὲς πολλὲς νὰ πᾶς,
νὰ μάθεις καὶ νὰ μάθεις ἀπ' τοὺς σπουδασμένους.

Πάντα στὸν νοῦ σου νἄχεις τὴν Ἰθάκη.
Τὸ φθάσιμον ἐκεῖ εἶν' ὁ προορισμός σου.
Ἀλλὰ μὴ βιάζεις τὸ ταξεῖδι διόλου.
Καλλίτερα χρόνια πολλὰ νὰ διαρκέσει·
καὶ γέρος πιὰ ν' ἀράξεις στὸ νησί,
πλούσιος μὲ ὅσα κέρδισες στὸν δρόμο,
μὴ προσδοκῶντας πλούτη νὰ σὲ δώσει ἡ Ἰθάκη.

Ἡ Ἰθάκη σ' ἔδωσε τ' ὡραῖο ταξεῖδι.
Χωρὶς αὐτὴν δὲν θἄβγαινες στὸν δρόμο.
Ἄλλα δὲν ἔχει νὰ σὲ δώσει πιά.

Κι ἂν πτωχικὴ τὴν βρεῖς, ἡ Ἰθάκη δὲν σὲ γέλασε.
Ἔτσι σοφὸς ποὺ ἔγινες, μὲ τόση πεῖρα,
ἤδη θὰ τὸ κατάλαβες ἡ Ἰθάκες τί σημαίνουν.

Ithaka
When you set out for Ithaka
ask that your way be long,
full of adventure, full of instruction.
The Laistrygonians and the Cyclops,
angry Poseidon—do not fear them:
such as these you will never find
as long as your thought is lofty, as long as a rare
emotion touch your spirit and your body.
The Laistrygonians and the Cyclops,
angry Poseidon—you will not meet them
unless you carry them in your soul,
unless your soul raise them up before you.

Ask that your way be long.
At many a summer dawn to enter
—with what gratitude, what joy—
ports seen for the first time;
to stop at Phoenician trading centres,
and to buy good merchandise,

mother of pearl and coral, amber and ebony,
and sensuous perfumes of every kind,
sensuous perfumes as lavishly as you can;
to visit many Egyptian cities,
to gather stores of knowledge from the learnèd.

Have Ithaka always in your mind.
Your arrival there is what you are destined for.
But don't in the least hurry the journey.
Better it last for years,
so that when you reach the island you are old,
rich with all you have gained on the way,
not expecting Ithaka to give you wealth.

Ithaka gave you the splendid journey.
Without her you would not have set out.
She hasn't anything else to give you.

And if you find her poor, Ithaka hasn't deceived you.
So wise have you become, of such experience,
that already you'll have understood what these Ithakas mean.

Translation by Rae Dalvern[32]

Ilias Venezis (1904–1973)

After the 1920s a new dimension was added to Greek writing by the tragic disaster in Asia Minor. Stratis Myrivilis, Ilias Venezis and Kosmas Politis are three writers associated with this period. Venezis was living in Ayvali on the coast of Asia Minor when in 1922 at the age of eighteen he was conscripted by the Turks into the compulsory working parties which were sent into the interior of Asia Minor. Venezis did not return to the coast until fourteen months later; he was lucky to survive. His novel *Number 31328* is a chronicle of his captivity. The extract given below is from the very beginning of the book. His language is the educated demotic that he himself would have spoken and the style is simple and unadorned to suit the serious nature of the content.

1922. Ἡ Ἀνατολὴ γλυκύτατη πάντα, γιὰ σονέτο—κάτι τέτοιο. Ὅλα ἦταν ἥμερα καὶ ἁβρὰ ἐκεῖνο τὸ φθινόπωρο. Ὁ ἐχτρὸς εἶχε κατεβῆ στὴν πόλη μας, τὸ Ἀϊβαλί. Καὶ στὸ λιμάνι εἶχαν ἀράξει βαπόρια μὲ ἀμερικάνικες παντιέρες.

The Twentieth Century: A Selection

Διαταγή: Τὸ σάπιο ἐμπόρευμα—τὰ παιδάκια κ' οἱ γυναῖκες—
θὰ μπαρκέρναν γιὰ τὴν Ἑλλάδα. Μὰ οἱ ἄντρες, ἀπὸ
δεκαοχτὼ ἴσαμε σαρανταπέντε χρονῶ, θὰ φεῦγαν γιὰ τὸ
ἐσωτερικό, σκλάβοι στὰ ἐργατικὰ τάγματα.
Ἡ εἴδηση ἔφερε ἕνα δυνατὸ τίναγμα στοὺς δικούς μας.
Τὰ ἐργατικὰ τάγματα ἦταν ἕνα μακρινὸ παρελθὸν ἀπ' τὸν
Μεγάλο Πόλεμο. Εἶχαν γίνει θρύλος. Χιλιάδες χριστιανοὶ
εἶχαν ἀφήσει στὰ κάτεργα αὐτὰ τὰ κόκαλά τους. Τὰ δάκρυα
στὶς μητέρες δὲν εἶχαν στερέψει ἀκόμα.
Γι' αὐτό, στὴν ἀρχή, κανένας ἀπ' τὰ νιάτα δὲν ἔβρισκε τὸ
κουράγιο νὰ παραδοθῆ. Μὰ σιγὰ-σιγὰ τὸ πῆραν ἀπόφαση.
Ἕναν μπόγο στὸ χέρι. Σὰ μαζεύουνταν διακόσοι-τρακόσοι
ἄνθρωποι, τοὺς στέλναν μὲ συνοδεία γιὰ τὸ ἐσωτερικό. Ἀπ'
τὴν ἄλλη, τὰ βαπόρια, ἀραιὰ-ἀραιὰ στὴν ἀρχή, ὕστερα
ὁλοένα πιὸ γεμάτα, ἄρχισαν νὰ βιάζουνται. Σφυρίζαν.
Πολλοὶ καπνοί. Οἱ γυναῖκες ξεπροβόδιζαν τοὺς ἄντρες τους,
ποὺ οἱ Τοῦρκοι τοὺς σέρναν στὸ ἐσωτερικὸ τῆς Ἀσίας, μὰ
νὰ μπαρκάρουν οἱ ἴδιες μὲ τ' ἀμερικάνικα δὲν τὸ ἀποφ-
άσιζαν. Μιὰ μέρα, δυὸ μέρες. Φοβοῦνταν πῶς ἔτσι τοὺς
ἐγκαταλείπουν. Ὅμως τὰ βαπόρια βγάζαν πολὺν καπνό.
Εἶχαν διορία, λίγες μέρες. Ὅποιος ἔμεινε, ἔμεινε. Σφυ-
ρίγματα, φωνές. Σιγὰ-σιγὰ ἡ θερμὴ ἀνάσα ξαπλώθηκε,
χίμηξε, ἀλάλιασε σ' ὅλες τὶς καρδιές. Ὅλοι ἄρχισαν νὰ
βιάζουνται.
Αὐτὸ εἶναι ὁ πανικός:
Ἤμουν δεκαοχτὼ χρονῶ. Δὲν ἤμουν ἐμπόρευμα γιὰ τὴν
Ἑλλάδα, μήτε μιὰ ὀκά· μήτε λίγο σάπιο πράμα—τίποτα.
Τὸ Νούμερο 31328: Κεφαλαῖο Α'

1922. Asia Minor, always so delightful, a theme for a sonnet, perhaps.
All was mild and still that autumn. The enemy had come down into our
city of Ayvali, while in the harbour were anchored boats flying American flags. The order was that the rotten merchandise, the women and
children, should embark for Greece but men aged between eighteen
and forty-five should leave for the interior to be slaves in the working
parties.
The news was a severe shock for our families. The working parties
were a distant memory from the Great War. They had become a
legend. Thousands of Christians had left their bones in those labour
camps. Their mothers' tears had still not dried.

This was the reason why, at first, none of the young men found the courage to present themselves. But gradually they made up their minds, each with a bundle of possessions in his hand. As two or three hundred gathered, they were sent with an escort to the interior. Behind them the boats began to hurry, sparsely-filled at first and then increasingly more packed. They were sounding their sirens and belching out smoke. The women saw off their menfolk whom the Turks were taking away into the interior of Asia Minor but they themselves could not make the decision to go on board the American boats. One day passed and then two. They were afraid that they were abandoning their men by embarking in this way. But the boats continued to belch forth smoke; they had been given only a few days in which to complete the evacuation. Whoever remained behind would stay for good. Whistles and shouts! Gradually everyone was caught up in the heat of the moment, a heat which spread around and rushed into their hearts and drove them to distraction. They all began to hurry.

Panic.

I was eighteen years old. I was not merchandise for Greece, not one oka; nor was I rotten material! I did not count!

Nikos Kazantzakis (1883–1957)

Kazantzakis was born in Heracleion, Crete, and studied Law in Athens and Paris. He was a traveller and a thinker who supplemented what he earned from his creative writings of poetry, prose and drama by doing translations and by writing school books. In 1918 and 1919 he worked for the Greek government, helping with the repatriation of Greeks from the Caucasus, but his subsequent communist allegiance, which developed after the fall of Venizelos, was to keep him at a distance from the Greek establishment for much of his life. The work which he himself considered the most important was his *Odyssey* which started with the hero's return to Ithaca and encompassed a whole new set of wanderings covering the full range of Kazantzakis' theories and ideas. Outside Greece, however, Kazantzakis is probably best known for his novels which have been widely translated. He wrote them after a thirty-three year period in which he had not written about modern Greece at all.

The extract given below is from his first novel, *The Life and Times of Alexis Zorbas*. The character of Zorba is based on a Greek with whom Kazantzakis worked in a mining enterprise in the Peloponnese from 1916 to 1917. Kazantzakis sets the action of the novel in Crete, however, and speaks through the person of a bookish narrator in admiration of the 'vital force' of the unconventional Zorba. The success of the book comes not only from its plot but also from the descriptive quality of the writing. All his life Kazantzakis was a serious campaigner for the use of demotic Greek and his language is a truly local version of this; much of the vocabulary and orthography is peculiar to himself.

Ἀνέβηκα σ' ἕνα ψήλωμα, κοίταξα. Αὐστηρό, σοβαρὸ τοπίο ἀπὸ σιδερόπετρα, ἀπὸ σκοῦρα δέντρα κι ἄσπρο ἀσβεστόχωμα ποὺ λὲς δὲν μπορεῖ κασμὰς νὰ τὸ χαράξει· μὰ ξάφνου κίτρινα ντελικάτα κρινάνθια τρυποῦσαν τὴν ἀστρακωμένη τούτη γῆς κι ἔλαμπαν στὸν ἥλιο. Μακριά, κατὰ νότου, ἕνα νησάκι χαμηλό, ἀμμουδερό, λαμποκοποῦσε τριανταφυλλένιο καὶ κοκκίνιζε καταπάρθενο στὶς πρῶτες ἀχτίδες.

Λίγο πιὸ μέσα ἀπὸ τὸ γυρογιάλι, ἐλιές, χαρουπιές, συκιές, λίγα ἀμπέλια· στὶς ἀπάνεμες λακκοῦβες, ἀνάμεσα σὲ δυὸ βουναλάκια, ξινόδεντρα καὶ μουσμουλιές, καὶ πιὸ κοντὰ στὸ γιαλό, τὰ μποστάνια.

Ὥρα πολλὴ χαίρουμουν ἀπὸ τὸ ψήλωμα τοὺς ἀπαλοὺς κυματισμοὺς τῆς γῆς· ζῶνες ζῶνες οἱ σιδερόπετρες, οἱ σκουροπράσινες χαρουπιές, οἱ ἀσημόφυλλες ἐλιές, σὰ ν' ἁπλώνουνταν μπροστά σου κυματιστὸ ριγάτο δέρμα τίγρης. Καὶ πέρα, κατὰ νότου, στραφτάλιζε ἡ θυμωμένη ἀκόμα θάλασσα, ἀπέραντη, ἔρημη, ἔφτανε ὣς τὴν Μπαρμπαριά, μούγκριζε, χιμοῦσε κι ἔτρωε τὴν Κρήτη.

Ἔμοιαζε τὸ κρητικὸ ἐτοῦτο τοπίο, ἔτσι μοῦ φάνηκε, μὲ τὴν καλὴ πρόζα: καλοδουλεμένο, λιγόλογο, λυτρωμένο ἀπὸ περιττὰ πλούτη, δυνατὸ καὶ συγκρατημένο. Διατύπωνε μὲ τ' ἁπλούστερα μέσα τὴν οὐσία. Δὲν ἔπαιζε, δὲν καταδέχουνταν νὰ χρησιμοποιήσει κανένα τερτίπι, δὲ ρητόρευε· ἔλεγε ὅ, τι ἤθελε νὰ πεῖ μὲ ἀντρίκια αὐστηρότητα. Μὰ ἀνάμεσα ἀπὸ τὶς αὐστηρὲς γραμμές του ξεχώριζες στὸ κρητικὸ ἐτοῦτο τοπίο ἀπροσδόκητη εὐαισθησία καὶ τρυφεράδα—σὲ ἀπάνεμες γοῦβες μοσκοβολοῦσαν οἱ λεμονιὲς κι οἱ πορτοκαλιές, καὶ πέρα, ἀπὸ τὴν ἀπέραντη θάλασσα, ξεχύνουνταν ἀστέρευτη ποίηση.

—Ἡ Κρήτη, μουρμούριζα, ἡ Κρήτη...—κι ἡ καρδιά μου ἀναπετάριζε.

from Βίος καὶ Πολιτεία τοῦ Ἀλέξη Ζορμπᾶ

I climbed a hill and looked around; a severe stern landscape of granite, dark trees and undentable white limestone. And yet, unexpectedly, delicate yellow lilies were pushing their way up through this blasted earth and were shining in the sun. Far off towards the south a small low sandy island gleamed with rosy hues and blushed shyly in the first rays of light.

A little way inland from the sea-shore were olive, carob and fig trees and a few vineyards. In the sheltered hollows between two small hills were citrus and loquat trees and nearer to the sea the vegetable plots.

I stood a long time there on that hill, rejoicing in the gentle undulations of the land; the granite in band after band, the dark-green carob trees, the silvery-leaved olive trees. I imagined a rippling striped tiger-skin spread out before me. And in the distance, to the south, sparkled the still-angry sea, boundless and deserted. It stretched out to Africa and roared, foamed and gnawed at Crete.

This Cretan landscape resembled good prose, I thought, carefully-composed, concise, free from excessive ornament, powerful and controlled. The impression it made came from its own simple vitality. It did not play games, it used no tricks of rhetoric; it said what it had to say with masculine severity. Yet, in the midst of its stern lines, this Cretan landscape also revealed an unexpected sensitivity and gentleness. In sheltered hollows there was the sweet scent of lemon and orange groves and further away an inexhaustible poetry flowed out from the boundless sea.

'Crete,' I murmured, 'Crete...' and my heart leapt up.

Pantelis Prevelakis (1909–86)

Prevelakis was born in Crete and had his general education there. Later he studied, worked and lived in Paris, Thessalonica and Athens. He is a distinguished academic and art historian. *The Chronicle of a City* is an account of his home town, Rethymnon, based on childhood memories before and after the exchange of populations in 1922. When he depicts the departure of the Muslims from Rethymnon it is a sad picture, for the Christian and Muslim communities had lived peacably side by side since independence at the end of the previous century.

The extract below tells how a bishop of Rethymnon prepared himself in order to paint an icon of the 'Pantocrator' in the church of St Barbara.

Ὁ Ἁγιογράφος

Νὰ ζωγραφίσεις μιὰν ἐκκλησιά, ἢ κ' ἕνα κόνισμα μονάχα,

εἶναι τέχνη ἱερή, ὄχι τέχνη σὰν τὶς ἄλλες. Ὁ χριστιανὸς ζωγράφος δὲν ξεχωρίζει ἀπὸ τὸν καλόγερο, κι ἆς ζεῖ μέσα στὶς πολιτεῖες, κι ἆς ἔχει πάρε-δῶσε μὲ τὸν κόσμο. "Οπως γονατίζει ὁ καλόγερος καὶ κάνει τὴν προσευκή του στὸ Θεό, ἔτσι κι ὁ ἁγιογράφος καθίζει στὸ σκαμνί του καὶ πιάνει τὰ κοντύλια του νὰ ζωγραφίσει. Προσευκὴ εἶναι κι αὐτουνοῦ ἡ δουλειά, μόνο ποὺ ἀντὶ νὰ μουρμουρίζει τὰ λόγια του, τὰ ζωγραφίζει. Πρέπει τὸ λοιπὸν νἄχει ἁγνὴ καρδιά, γλῶσσα ἀμόλευτη ἀπὸ αἰσχρά, χέρια παστρικὰ καὶ κορμὶ ἀγυναίκιστο. Πρὶ νὰ πιάσει τὰ κοντύλια του καὶ τὶς μπογιές, χρέος ἔχει νὰ ἑτοιμαστεῖ, νὰ νηστέψει, νὰ διαβάσει τὸ συναξάρι τοῦ ἁγίου ποὺ θὰ στορίσει καὶ νὰ μπεῖ μέσα στὴ ζωὴ καὶ στὸ μαρτύριό του. Ἡ ψυχή του πρέπει νἆναι καθαρὴ σὰν τὸ κρούσταλο, καὶ τότε μόνο θὰ πέσει ἀπάνω του ἡ θεία χάρη καὶ θὰ κατέβει ἀπ' τὸ κοντύλι του ἡ ἅγια εἰκόνα. Δὲν ἔχει ἐδῶ νὰ καυκηθεῖ ὁ ζωγράφος μὲ τὸ ἔργο του, οὔτε νὰ βάλει μέσα σ' αὐτὸ πράματα ἢ φροντίδες ἀπὸ τὴ ζωή του, ὅπως κάνουν ἀλλοῦ, ποὺ θὰ δεῖς τὴν ξεστήθωτη παλλακὴ νὰ κάνει τὴν Παναγιά. Ἐδῶ ἡ εἰκόνα εἶναι χάρισμα τοῦ Θεοῦ, κι ὁ ζωγράφος εἶναι χάρισμα τοῦ Θεοῦ, κι ὁ ζωγράφος εἶναι ὁ ἀγωγὸς τῆς πνοῆς Του. Μόνο ἡ νήστεια, ἡ ἁγνότητα κ' ἡ ὑποταγὴ κάνουν τὸ "Αγιο Πνεῦμα νὰ ἐπιφοιτήσει στὸ κεφάλι τοῦ δούλου τοῦ Θεοῦ καὶ μόνο μὲ τὴ χάρη Του γίνεται τὸ ἄξιο ἔργο, ἀπὸ ψυχὴ ποὺ σκιρτᾶ ἀπὸ μακαριότητα καὶ βνωμοσύνη. Γιὰ τοῦτο, ὁ ζωγράφος δὲ θὰ βάλει ποτὲ τὄνομά του στὴν εἰκόνα, οὔτε θὰ διαλαλήσει μιὰ δόξα ποὺ δὲν εἶναι δική του. Κι ἂν γίνει ἐξαίρεση ἀπὸ τοῦτο, τὄνομά του θὰ τὄχει ταπεινὰ σημαδεμένο σὲ καμιὰ γωνιά, ὄχι γιὰ τὴ δόξα του μέσα στὸν κόσμο, παρὰ σὰ δέηση στὰ πόδια τοῦ Κυρίου.

Ὁ δεσπότης ὁ Ἱερόθεος, ὁ μεγάλος ἱεράρχης, πρὶ νὰ πιάσει νὰ ζωγραφίζει τὸν Παντοκράτορα στὸ θόλο τῆς Ἁγια-Βαρβάρας, νήστεψε δυὸ βδομάδες καὶ προετοιμάστηκε σὰ νἄχε νὰ μεταλάβει. Στὴν τρίτη βδομάδα, ἀνέβηκε πάνω στὴ σκαλωσιά, μὲ τὶς μπογιὲς καὶ τὰ κοντύλια του, κ' ἔβαλε ἀρχή.

...

...

Ὁ Μεγαλοδύναμος ἀγρίευε ὥρα τὴν ὥρα, τὰ φρύδια Του ζαρώναν, τὰ μάτια Του πετοῦσανε φωτιές, λοξοτηρώντας. Ὁ δεσπότης λιγόστευε κοντά Του, σούρωνε, μαύριζε τὸ πετσί του ἀπὸ τὴν ἀδυναμιά. Ὁ ἀγώνας του βάστηξε ἔντεκα μέρες. Στὴ δωδέκατη, ὁ ταξιμάρης δεσπότης κατέβηκε στὴ γῆς, ἔκαμε νὰ περπατήσει, κουφογονάτισε. Τὰ νεῦρα τοῦ λαιμοῦ του εἴχανε πιαστεῖ, τὰ μάτια του δὲν ἔβλεπαν στὰ ἴσια, ἡ θέρμη τοὔκαιγε τὸ κορμί. Μιὰ βδομάδα ἀκόμα εἴχε νὰ κάνει μὲ τὸ Θεό. Ξημέρωμα Κυριακῆς, σηκώθηκε ἀπὸ τὸ στρῶμα, νίφτηκε, ἔβγαλε τοὺς ἀσβέστες ἀπὸ τὰ γένια του καὶ πῆγε νὰ λειτουργήσει στὴν Ἁγια-Βαρβάρα. Ὅμως ἡ καρδιά του δὲν τὄλεγε νὰ κοιτάξει τἀψήλου. Μόνο σὰν ἦρθε στὸ μέρος ἐκεῖνο τῆς ἀκολουθίας ποὺ ὁ λειτουργὸς βγαίνει στὴ βασιλόπορτα καὶ δέεται, ὁ δεσπότης ἀναβλεμμάτισε στὸ ἔργο ποὺ ὁ Κύριος ἔιχε εὐδοκήσει νὰ ἐχτελέσει μὲ τὸ χέρι τοῦ δούλου Του. Τὸ μέτωπό του παχνίστηκε, τὰ χέρια του πήρανε νὰ τρέμουν, καὶ τὰ δάκρυα πηδήσαν ἀπὸ τὰ μάτια του... Κι ὅλο τὸ ἐκκλησίασμα ἔκλαιε μαζί του, κ' εἴταν ἀνείπωτα, ριζόκορφα εὐτυχισμένο πλάι στὸ βοσκό του.

from Τὸ Χρονικὸ Μίας Πολιτείας

The Icon Painter

To paint a church, or even simply an icon, is a sacred art, unlike any other. The Christian painter is no different from a monk, even though he may live in society and have dealings with the world. Just as the monk kneels and says his prayers to God, so the icon painter sits on his stool and takes up his brushes to make his drawing. Prayer is his work too, only instead of reciting the words, he paints them. Therefore he must have a pure heart, an unsullied tongue and clean hands and he must be celibate. Before taking up his brushes and paints he needs to prepare himself, to fast, to read the Book of the Saint whom he is about to portray and to enter into his life and martyrdom. His soul ought to be pure as snow, for only then will he be filled with the divine grace and only then will the holy icon grow from under his brush.

Here the painter must not grow proud of his painting nor introduce into it his own experiences or thoughts, as they do elsewhere (getting a buxom wench to represent the Virgin Mary). Here the icon is a gift of God and the painter is the channel of His inspiration. Only fasting, purity and obedience can make the Holy Spirit come down into the mind of God's servant and only through His grace is the divine work accomplished by a soul abundantly blessed and favoured. For this reason the painter will never put his name on the icon nor will he boast of a glory that is not his own. If there is an exception to this, he will have his name modestly noted in a corner, not for his own glory but as a mark of supplication before the Lord.

The bishop Hierotheos, the great prelate, before starting to paint his God the Almighty in the dome of the church of Saint Barbara fasted for two weeks and prepared himself as if to give Holy Communion. When the third week came, he went up on to the scaffolding with his paints and his brushes and he made a start...

...

... The Almighty was growing fiercer every hour. He was knitting his brows and His eyes were flashing fire, looking down askance. The bishop shrank beside Him. All his strength was draining away and his face was grey with tiredness. His struggle lasted for eleven days. On the twelfth, the devoted bishop came down to the ground. He tried to walk but collapsed on to his knees. The muscles of his neck had become stiff, he could not see straight and his body was burning with fever. He had one more week to spend with his God. On the Sunday morning he got up from his bed, washed, combed the lime out of his beard and went to say mass in the church of Saint Barbara. Yet he had not the courage to look on high. When he came to that part of the service when the officiant goes to the altar screen and prays, only then did the bishop look up at the work which the Lord had been pleased to accomplish by His servant's hand. His face stiffened, his hands began to shake and the tears leapt forth from his eyes. And all the congregation were weeping with him and were speechless with great joy alongside their shepherd.

George Seferis (1900–71)

Seferis was born in Smyrna but moved to Athens before the Asia Minor catastrophe. After studying in Paris he followed a successful career in the Greek Diplomatic Service. Alongside his career and throughout his life he produced a great output of poetry, essays and translations. His poetry looks at the fate of man in relation to the ancient past and the natural world in which he lives. It is pervaded by a sense of beauty and a sense of sorrow. Seferis' ability to use images from the past is well illustrated in *The King of Asine*. We know of this king from a single phrase in Homer's Iliad; we know where his citadel was. But now he is only 'a void beneath the mask'. The first part of this poem is given below.[33]

Ὁ Βασιλιὰς τῆς Ἀσίνης
Κοιτάξαμε ὅλο τὸ πρωὶ γύρω-γύρω τὸ κάστρο

97

ἀρχίζοντας ἀπὸ τὸ μέρος τοῦ ἴσκιου ἐκεῖ ποὺ ἡ θάλασσα
πράσινη καὶ χωρὶς ἀναλαμπή, τὸ στῆθος σκοτωμένου
                             παγονιοῦ
μᾶς δέχτηκε ὅπως ὁ καιρὸς χωρὶς κανένα χάσμα.
Οἱ φλέβες τοῦ βράχου κατέβαιναν ἀπὸ ψηλὰ
στριμμένα κλήματα γυμνὰ πολύκλωνα ζωντανεύοντας
στ' ἄγγιγμα τοῦ νεροῦ, καθὼς τὸ μάτι ἀκολουθώντας τις
πάλευε νὰ ξεφύγει τὸ κουραστικὸ λίκνισμα
χάνοντας δύναμη ὁλοένα.

'Απὸ τὸ μέρος τοῦ ἥλιου ἕνας μακρὺς ὁλάνοιχτος
καὶ τὸ φῶς τρίβοντας διαμαντικὰ στὰ μεγάλα τείχη.
Κανένα πλάσμα ζωντανὸ τ' ἀγριοπερίστερα φευγάτα
κι ὁ βασιλιὰς τῆς 'Ασίνης ποὺ τὸν γυρεύουμε δυὸ χρόνια
                             τώρα
ἄγνωστος λησμονημένος ἀπ' ὅλους κι ἀπὸ τὸν "Ομηρο
μόνο μιὰ λέξη στὴν 'Ιλιάδα κι ἐκείνη ἀβέβαιη
ριγμένη ἐδῶ σὰν τὴν ἐντάφια χρυσὴ προσωπίδα.
Τὴν ἄγγιξες, θυμᾶσαι τὸν ἦχο της; κούφιο μέσα στὸ φῶς
σὰν τὸ στεγνὸ πιθάρι στὸ σκαμμένο χῶμα·
κι ὁ ἴδιος ἦχος μὲς στὴ θάλασσα μὲ τὰ κουπιά μας.
'Ο βασιλιὰς τῆς 'Ασίνης ἕνα κενὸ κάτω ἀπ' τὴν προσωπίδα
παντοῦ μαζί μας παντοῦ μαζί μας, κάτω ἀπὸ ἕνα ὄνομα:
" 'Ασίνην τε... 'Ασίνην τε... "
               καὶ τὰ παιδιά του ἀγάλματα
κι οἱ πόθοι του φτερουγίσματα πουλιῶν κι ὁ ἀγέρας
στὰ διαστήματα τῶν στοχασμῶν του καὶ τὰ καράβια του
ἀραγμένα σ' ἄφαντο λιμάνι·
κάτω ἀπ' τὴν προσωπίδα ἕνα κενό.
...
...

The King of Asine
We looked all morning round the citadel
starting from the shaded side, there where the sea,
green and without reflection—breast of a slain peacock—
accepted us like time without a single gap.
The veins of rock descended from high above,
twisted vines, naked, many-branched, coming alive
at the touch of water, while the eye following them

98

fought to escape the tiresome rocking,
losing strength continually.

On the sunny side, a long open beach
and the light striking diamonds on the large walls.
No living thing, the wild doves gone
and the King of Asine, whom we have been searching for two years
                                                                    now,
unknown, forgotten by all, even by Homer,
only one word in the 'Iliad' and that uncertain,
thrown there like the gold burial mask.
You touched it, remember its sound? Hollow in the light
like a dry jar in dug earth:
the same sound that our oars make in the sea.
The King of Asine a void beneath the mask
everywhere with us everywhere with us, behind a single phrase:
' 'Ασίνην τε... 'Ασίνην τε...'
                          and his children statues
and his desires the fluttering of birds, and the wind
in the interstices of his thoughts, and his ships
anchored in a vanished port:
beneath the mask a void.
...
...

Translated by E. Keeley and P. Sherrard[34]

Odysseus Elytis (born 1911)
Elytis' early poetry was optimistic and dreamlike. He exulted in the
landscape and climate of Greece. After his experiences in the war in
Albania in 1940, he became more serious. In 1960 he published Tò
"Αξιον 'Εστί, *Worthy it is*, the title of a Byzantine hymn in honour of the
Virgin Mary ('Worthy it is to magnify thee, Mother of God'—the Arch-
angel Gabriel's words of annunciation to Mary). It is a long poem in three
parts, 'Η Γένεσις (Genesis), Τὰ Πάθη (Passion) and Tò
Δοξαστικόν(Gloria). The beautiful language has echoes of Homer, Solo-
mos and the Orthodox Church.
    The first extract is from 'Genesis'. The stages of creation are seen as
the ages of man and are represented by the hours from dawn to mid-day.
The passage given below is from the third hour. The second extract is
Psalm Two of The Passion and it records the importance of language for

a poet. In both extracts there is a deliberate patterning of language and use of a refrain. Colour, light and images of the Aegean are also characteristically present.[35]

From Ἡ Γένεσις

'Κάθε λέξη κι ἀπὸ 'να χελιδόνι
γιὰ νὰ σοῦ φέρνει τὴν ἄνοιξη μέσα στὸ θέρος ' εἶπε
Καὶ πολλὰ τὰ λιόδεντρα
    ποὺ νὰ κρησάρουν στὰ χέρια τους τὸ φῶς
    κι ἐλαφρὸ ν' ἁπλώνεται στὸν ὕπνο σου
καὶ πολλὰ τὰ τζιτζίκια
    ποὺ νὰ μὴν τὰ νιώθεις
    ὅπως δὲ νιώθεις τὸ σφυγμὸ χέρι στὸ σου
ἀλλὰ λίγο τὸ νερὸ
    γιὰ νὰ τό 'χεις Θεὸ καὶ νὰ κατέχεις τί σημαίνει
                           ὁ λόγος του
καὶ το δέντρο μονάχο του
    χωρὶς κοπάδι
    γιὰ νὰ τὸ κάνεις φίλο σου
    καὶ νὰ γνωρίζεις τ' ακριβό του τ' ὄνομα
φτενὸ στὰ πόδια σου τὸ χῶμα
    γιὰ νὰ μὴν ἔχεις ποῦ ν' ἁπλώσεις ρίζα
    καὶ νὰ τραβᾶς τοῦ βάθους ὁλοένα
καὶ πλατὺς ἐπάνου ὁ οὐρανὸς
    γιὰ νὰ διαβάζεις μόνος σου τὴν ἀπεραντοσύνη
                     ΑΥΤΟΣ
           ὁ κόσμος ὁ μικρός, ὁ μέγας!

'Each word a swallow
to bring you spring in the midst of summer,' he said
And ample the olive trees
    to sift the light through their fingers
    that it may spread gently over your sleep
and ample the cicadas
    which you will feel no more
    than you feel the pulse inside your wrist
but scarce the water
    so that you hold it a God and understand the meaning of its voice
and the tree alone
    no flock beneath it

so that you take it for a friend
and know its precious name
sparse the earth beneath your feet
so that you have no room to spread your roots
and keep reaching down in depth
and broad the sky above
so that you read the infinite on your own
THIS WORLD
this small world the great!
Translated by E. Keeley and G. Savidis

From Τὰ Πάθη

B'

Τὴ γλώσσα μοῦ ἔδωσαν ἑλληνική·
τὸ σπίτι φτωχικὸ στὶς ἀμμουδιὲς τοῦ Ὁμήρου.
Μονάχη ἔγνοια ἡ γλώσσα μου στὶς ἀμμουδιὲς τοῦ
Ὁμήρου.
Ἐκεῖ σπάροι καὶ πέρκες
ἀνεμόδαρτα ῥήματα
ρεύματα πράσινα μὲς στὰ γαλάζια
ὅσα εἶδα στὰ σπλάχνα μου ν' ἀνάβουνε
σφουγγάρια, μέδουσες
μὲ τὰ πρῶτα λόγια τῶν Σειρήνων
ὄστρακα ῥόδινα μὲ τὰ πρῶτα μαῦρα ρίγη.
Μονάχη ἔγνοια ἡ γλώσσα μου μὲ τὰ πρῶτα μαῦρα ρίγη.
Ἐκεῖ ῥόδια, κυδώνια
θεοὶ μελαχρινοί, θεῖοι κι ἐξάδελφοι
τὸ λάδι ἀδειάζοντας μὲς στὰ πελώρια κιούπια·
καὶ πνοὲς ἀπὸ τὴ ρεματιὰ εὐωδιάζοντας
λυγαριὰ καὶ σχίνο
σπάρτο καὶ πιπερόριζα
μὲ τὰ πρῶτα πιπίσματα τῶν σπίνων,
ψαλμωδίες γλυκὲς μὲ τὰ πρῶτα-πρῶτα Δόξα Σοι.
Μονάχη ἔγνοια ἡ γλώσσα μου, μὲ τὰ πρῶτα-πρῶτα Δόξα Σοι!
Ἐκεῖ δάφνες καὶ βάγια
θυμιατὸ καὶ λιβάνισμα
τὶς πάλες εὐλογώντας καὶ τὰ καριοφίλια.
Στὸ χῶμα τὸ στρωμένο μὲ τ' ἀμπελομάντιλα
κνίσες, τσουγκρίσματα
καὶ Χριστὸς Ἀνέστη

101

μὲ τὰ πρῶτα σμπάρα τῶν Ἑλλήνων.
᾽Αγάπες μυστικὲς μὲ τὰ πρῶτα λόγια τοῦ Ὕμνου.
Μονάχη ἔγνοια ἡ γλώσσα μου, μὲ τὰ πρῶτα λόγια τοῦ
Ὕμνου!

Greek the language they gave me;
poor the house on Homer's shores.
My only care my language on Homer's shores.
There bream and perch
windbeaten verbs,
green sea currents in the blue,
all I saw light up in my entrails,
sponges, jellyfish
with the first words of the Sirens,
rosy shells with the first black shivers.
My only care my language with the first black shivers.
There pomegranates, quinces,
swarthy gods, uncles and cousins
emptying oil into giant jars;
and breaths from the ravine fragrant
with osier and terebinth
broom and ginger root
with the first chirping of finches,
sweet psalms with the very first Glory Be to Thee.
My only care the language with the very first Glory Be to Thee!
There laurel and palm leaves
censer and incense
blessing the swords and muskets.
On soil spread with vine-scarves,
the smell of roasting lamb, Easter eggs cracking,
and 'Christ is Risen',
with the first salvos of the Greeks.
Secret loves with the first words of the Hymn.
My only care my language with the first words of the Hymn!

Translated by E. Keeley and G. Savidis

N.B.
1. The customs of the Greek Orthodox Easter include the roasting of lamb, the cracking of coloured eggs, by striking the tip of one against the other, and the greeting Χριστὸς ᾽Ανέστη (Christ is Risen) to which is given the reply ᾽Αληθῶς ᾽Ανέστη (He is risen indeed).

2. The 'Hymn' refers to Solomos' *Hymn to Liberty*.

Antonis Samarakis (born 1919)

Samarakis' novel Τὸ Λάθος *The Flaw* was written in 1965 and won world-wide acclaim. Two police agents accompany a suspect and act out an elaborate charade which is intended to trap him into revealing himself. The reader follows the developing relationship between the suspect and one of the agents in particular. The setting for the story is an undefined totalitarian regime but the main interest is in the psychological drama.

The extract below is from the final pages of the novel. The agent who has spent most time with the suspect has had a change of heart and is now encouraging him to escape. The language is loosely structured and totally modern but the simple approach, which is characteristic of the whole novel, is very much a cover for the underlying subtleties and ironies of the plot.

Δὲν μπορῶ νὰ τὸν παραδώσω, τὸ Σχέδιο, τὸ τέλειο Σχέδιο εἶναι σὰν ἕνα "τέλειο ἔγκλημα " ποὺ δὲν εἶναι "τέλειο ", ὅλα τὰ εἴχαμε προβλέψει μὲ κάθε λεπτομέρεια, ὅλα τὰ εἴχαμε ὑπολογίσει μὲ μαθηματικὴ ἀκρίβεια, ὅλα τὰεἴχαμε ἀριστοτεχνικὰ ἐκτελέσει, ὅμως ἔγινε ἕνα λάθος, ἕνα λάθος καὶ δὲν προφταίνω αὐτὴν τὴ στιγμὴ νὰ σκεφτῶ περ- ισσότερα, ὁ μάνατζερ μοῦ καρφώνει τὴ ματιά του, δὲν πιστεύει ὅ, τι βλέπει, ὅ, τι ἀκούει, ἐγώ, ὁ ἀνακριτὴς τῆς Εἰδικῆς Ὑπηρεσίας, ὁ ἔμπιστος τοῦ Καθεστῶτος, ὁ φανα- τικὸς τοῦ Καθεστῶτος, ἐγὼ εἶμαι ποὺ λέω στὸν κρατούμενο *Φύγε!* καὶ προσπαθῶ νὰ τὸν κάνω νὰ δραπετεύσει, ὁ μάνατζερ βέβαια δὲν ὑποψιάζεται τί συνέβη μέσα μου, τὸ Καθεστὼς δὲν εἶναι πιὰ σὲ πρῶτο πλάνο στὴ συνείδησή μου, στὴν καρδιά μου, ὁ ἄνθρωπος στὴ μαρκίζα εἶναι σὲ πρῶτο πλάνο, ἐγὼ καὶ ὁ ἄνθρωπος τῆς μαρκίζας εἴμαστε παρέα, μιὰ βόλτα οἱ δυό μας στὴν πόλη, μιὰ βόλτα οἱ δυό μας στὴ ζωή, δεμένοι ὁ ἕνας μὲ τὸν ἄλλον μὲ κάτι ποὺ δὲν τὸ εἴχαμε στὴν Εἰδικὴ Ὑπηρεσία προϋπολογίσει, στὸ Σχέδιο ὑπάρχει ἕνα λάθος, στὸ Καθεστὼς ὑπάρχει ἕνα λάθος, ὄχι, οἱ ἄνθρωποι δὲ χωρίζονται σ' ἐκείνους ποὺ εἶναι μὲ τὸ Καθεστὼς καὶ σ' ἐκείνους ποὺ δὲν εἶναι μὲ τὸ Καθεστώς, ἕνα λάθος, κρίσιμο λάθος ἔχουμε κάνει, τὸ Καθεστὼς εἶναι διάτρητο ἀπὸ τὸ ἕνα τοῦτο λάθος, ἕνα λάθος-δυναμίτη ποὺ θὰ μᾶς τινάξει στὸν ἀέρα, δὲν μπορῶ νὰ τὸν παραδώσω,

εἶμαι σὲ θέση νὰ ξέρω τί μὲ περιμένει, ὅμως δὲ θὰ τὸν παραδώσω, δὲ θὰ τὸν προδώσω τὸν ἄλλον αὐτὸν ἄνθρωπο ποὺ μὲ κοιτάζει ἀπὸ τρία μέτρα ἀπόσταση, γαντζωμένος στὴ μαρκίζα, γαντζωμένος πάνω μου, ἕνα λάθος κυκλοφορεῖ παρ- άνομα σὲ ὅ, τι θεωρούσαμε σίγουρο καὶ ἀπαρασάλευτο, ἕνα λάθος εἶναι κάπου ἐδῶ γύρω μας, μέσα μας, ἕνα λάθος
—Φύγε !

I can't hand him over; the Plan, the perfect Plan, is like a 'perfect crime' which isn't perfect; we had foreseen every eventuality in every detail, we had calculated everything with a mathematical accuracy and we had carried everything out superbly; yet there turned out to be a flaw, yes a flaw, and I haven't time at this minute to think any more about it; the manager is glaring at me; he doesn't believe what he sees or what he hears; I, the interrogator of the Special Service, I, the loyal servant of the Regime, the enthusiastic supporter of the Regime, I am the man who is saying to the detainee 'Escape!' and I am trying to get him to escape; the manager, of course, has no idea what has happened to me; the Regime is no longer the first thing on my mind, it is no longer in my heart; the man on the ledge is my first thought; the man on the ledge and I are companions; the two of us took a walk together in the city, the two of us took a walk in life, bound one to the other by something that we in the Special Service had not foreseen; there is a flaw in the Plan, a flaw in the Regime; men cannot be divided into those who are with the Regime and those who are not with the Regime; we have made a mistake, a critical mistake; the Regime is marred by this one flaw, one flaw which is dynamite to blow us sky-high; I cannot hand him over; I know full well the fate that awaits me, nevertheless I shall not hand him over;I shall not hand over the other human being who watches me from a distance of three metres, clinging to the ledge, depending on me; contrary to all the rules, one flaw undermines all that we thought was sure and unshakable; there is a flaw, around us, inside us, a flaw.
'Escape!'

NOTES

CHAPTER 1

1. J. Chadwick *The Decipherment of Linear B* (1967).
2. J.T. Hooker *Linear B, An Introduction* (1980).
3. J. Chadwick *The Decipherment of Linear B* (1967).
4. Herodotus I. 57.
5. For a fuller discussion of this whole topic with reference to recent research, see L.R. Palmer *The Greek Language* (1980) Chapter 1.
6. For fuller details on the dialects see C.D. Buck *The Greek Dialects* (1955) and L.R. Palmer *The Greek Language* (1980).

CHAPTER 2

7. R. Browning *Medieval and Modern Greek* (1983).
8. B.P. Grenfell and A.S. Hunt *Oxyrhynchus Papyri* Part II (1899).
9. A.S. Hunt and C.C. Edgar *Select Papyri* (Loeb, 1932).
10. The texts of letters 1 and 2 are from the BGU archives (Museum of Berlin).
11. Translation from *The New English Bible* (1961).
12. Translation from *The New English Bible* (1961).
13. Translation from *The Penguin Book of Greek Verse* Trypanis (1971).
14. Translation by R.J.H. Jenkins (1967).
15. Arnold Toynbee *Constantine Porphyrogenitus and His World* (1973).
16. From Τριανταφυλλίδης Νεοελληνική Γραμματική (1941).

CHAPTER 3

17. Quoted by Michael Llewellyn Smith *The Great Island* (1965).
18. C.M. Woodhouse *The Greek War of Independence* (1952).
19. Κρητικὲς Μαντινάδες τοῦ Γιάννη Ε. Δερμιτζάκη. Σητεία (1963).
20. Roderick Beaton *Folk Poetry of Modern Greece* (1980).
21. Roderick Beaton *Folk Poetry of Modern Greece* (1980).
22. The three extracts in this section and their translations are from *The Penguin Book of Greek Verse*, edited by C.A. Trypanis (1971).

CHAPTER 4

23. Peter Bien *Kazantzakis and the Linguistic Revolution in Greek Literature* (1972).

105

24. Translation from the New English Bible (1961).

25. Makriyannis: edited and translated by H.A. Lidderdale (1966).

26. Translation by H.A. Lidderdale, op. cit.

27. Translation by Sir Compton Mackenzie *Wind of Freedom* (1944).

CHAPTER V

28. Many more names could be added, particularly those of recent prose writers. Useful summaries of the period can be found in two histories of modern Greek literature which have been translated into English, one by L. Politis (1973) and the other by C.T. Dimaras (1974).

29. Kostis Palamas *The Twelve Lays of the Gipsy*, translated by George Thomson (1969).

30. Peter Bien *Constantine Cavafy* (1964).

31. Edmund Keeley and Philip Sherrard *Four Greek Poets* (1966).

32. From *Four Greek Poets*, op. cit.

33. A fuller discussion of this poem can be found in *The Marble Threshing Floor* by Philip Sherrard (1955,1980) and in *Six Poets of Modern Greece* by Edmund Keeley and Philip Sherrard (1960).

34. Cf. footnote 33.

35. For a full discussion of this poem, read *The Axion Esti* translated and annotated by Edmund Keeley and George Savidis (1980). This work is also the source of the translations which follow.

APPENDIX ONE
LINEAR B

The following **rules of orthography** have been established:[†]
N.B. English letters represent the sounds of Linear B.
1. Five vowels (a, e, i, o, u), but length not indicated.
2. The second component of diphthongs in –u is indicated by a separate sign, e.g. qa–si–re–u = βασιλεύς.
3. The second component of diphthongs in –i is usually omitted, e.g. po–me = ποιμήν, o–no = ὄνοι.
4. 'j' represents a glide between certain vowels, e.g. i–je–re–u = ἱερεύς, po–ti–ni–ja = πότνια.
5. Twelve consonants:
    j (as above)
    w (digamma) e.g. ne–wo = νέϝος
    d, m, n, s = δ, μ, ν, σ
    k used for κ, χ, γ e.g. ki–to = χιτών
    p used for π, φ, β
    t used for τ, θ e.g. te–o = θεός
    r is an arbitrary transcription for the sign representing either ρ or λ, e.g. do–e–ro = δόελος (δοῦλος)
    z = ζ
    q used for the labio-velars, kʷ, gʷ, which had changed by the classical period into some of the sounds represented by β, δ, π, φ, τ and θ, e.g. e–qe–ta = ἑπέτᾱς, qe = τε and qa–si–re–u = βασιλεύς
6. No sign for the aspirate.
7. A consonant at the end of a syllable is not represented e.g. ka–ko = χαλκός, a–pi = ἀμφί, pa–te = πατήρ.
8. Initial 's' is omitted before a consonant, e.g. pe–mo/pe–ma = σπέρμο/σπέρμα.
9. A 'stop' consonant preceding another consonant is written with the vowel of the following syllable, e.g. ku–ru–so = χρυσός, a–mi–ni–so = Ἀμνισός.
N.B. There are syllabic signs for both vowels on their own and for consonants followed by vowels.

† Based on the table given by John Chadwick in *The Decipherment of Linear B* (1967).

Ideograms[†]
The following are some of the more detailed ideograms:

—man   —woman

—horse

—tripod

—wheel

—arrow

—sword (dagger)

Ideograms present vessels with different numbers of handles and the accompanying syllabograms usually refer to this as a number of 'ears'.

o–we represents the Greek word for ear *ὀϝός (Attic οὖς)

e.g.   qe–to–ro–we = τετρῶϝες —four-handled

ti–ri–o–we = τριῶϝες —three-handled

There are separate **signs for weights and measures**, and **numerals** are expressed as follows:

10,000   1,000   100   10 | 1

Therefore 1509 is written

† Taken from J.T. Hooker *Linear B, An Introduction* (1983).

APPENDIX TWO
THE GREEK ALPHABET

Semitic Name	Greek Name	
ảleph	ἄλφα	A
beth	βῆτα	B
gimel	γάμμα	Γ
daleth	δέλτα	Δ
he	εἶ (later ἔψιλον)	E
waw (vau)	(see note below)	
zayin (tsade)	ζῆτα	Z
cheth	ῆτα	H
teth	θῆτα	Θ
yod	ἰῶτα	I
kaph	κάππα	K
lamedh	λάμβδα	Λ
mem	μῦ	M
nun	νῦ	N
samech	ξεῖ	Ξ
ảyin	οὖ (later ὄμικρον)	O
pe	πεῖ	Π
qoph	(see note below)	
resh	ῥῶ	P
shin	σίγμα	Σ
taw	ταῦ	T
	ὕψιλον (see note below on 'waw')	
	φεῖ	Φ
	χεῖ	X
	ψεῖ	Ψ
	ὦμεγα	Ω

'waw' was given two forms: one was used for the vowel u (upsilon), and the other Ϝ (digamma) was believed to be a 'w' sound. In the Cypriot and Mycenaean syllabaries there are signs for Wa, We, Wi and Wo but in the Attic dialect it was lost at an early date. In Homer it accounts for the absence of elision in certain places and it played an important part in the metre of non-Attic poetry.

'qoph' represents a 'qi' sound. The sign for it is found in the oldest Attic inscriptions but it went out of use at an early date, the sign existing only as a numeral. It did, however, survive in the western version of the Greek alphabet and thence as the q of Latin.

APPENDIX THREE
INDO-EUROPEAN LANGUAGES

The Indo-European languages have traditionally been divided into two major groups, a western group which pronounces k and c as hard sounds and an eastern group which softens these letters to sibilants. These two groups are sometimes referred to as the 'centum' and 'satǝm' groups because of the different pronunciation of the words for one hundred, as shown in the diagram below.[†]

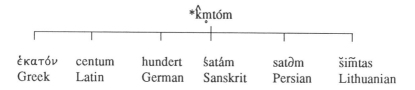

ἑκατόν	centum	hundert	śatám	satǝm	šim̃tas
Greek	Latin	German	Sanskrit	Persian	Lithuanian

Thus a table such as the following can be drawn up:

Original Indo-European

Western Languages (centum)	Easter languages (satǝm)
Greek	Indo-Iranian
Italic (Latin, Oscan, Umbrian)	(including Sanskrit)
Germanic	Armenian
Celtic	Baltic/Slavonic
Hittite	Albanian
Tocharian (Chinese Turkestan)	

Greek, however, although classed as a western language, is in fact much closer to certain 'satǝm' languages, such as Armenian and Indo-Iranian, than to the 'centum' languages, despite its subsequent cultural association with the West. Hittite and Tocharian, on the other hand, although classified as western, did not belong to the West geographically. It is also worth noting that the Indo-European family does not include all the European

† Γ.Δ. Μπαμπινιώτης Συνοπτική Ἱστορία τῆς Ἑλληνικῆς Γλώσσας (1985).

111

languages. Among the exceptions are Finnish, Hungarian and Basque. English is classed with the Germanic languages but has also, through French influence, been affected by the Romance languages which descended from Latin.

The following table gives some examples of synonyms and similarities of inflection in Indo-European languages:

I.E.	Greek	Latin	Sanskrit	German	English
*duo/dwō	δύο	duo	dvā	zwei	two
*tri/treyes	τρεῖς	trēs	trayas	drei	three
*e(me)	ἐμέ	me	mam	mich	me
*mātēr	μήτηρ (Dor. μάτερ)	mātĕr	mātā	mutter	mother
*pɘtēr	πατήρ	pater	pitā	vater	father
*es–mi	εἰμί	sum	as–mi	ich bin	
*es–si	εἶ (ἐσ–σί)	es	asi	sie sind	
*es–ti	ἐστί	est	as–ti	er ist	
*s–mes/ s–mos	ἐσμέν (Dor. εἰμές)	sumus	s–mas	wir sind	
*s–te	ἐσ–τέ	estis	s–tha	sie sind	
*se–nti	εἰσί (Dor. ἐντί)	sunt	s–anti	sie sind	

APPENDIX FOUR
THE PRONUNCIATION OF MODERN GREEK

The phonetic symbol is given and an English equivalent is suggested.

α	(a)	cat
β	(v)	verse
γ	(gh)	sugar
(before i & e sounds)	(y)	yes
δ	(dh)	that
ε	(e)	ten
ζ	(z)	haze
η	(i)	meet
θ	(th)	think
ι	(i)	meet
κ	(k)	king
λ	(l)	love
μ	(m)	may
ν	(n)	not
ξ	(ks)	box
ο	(ɔ)	bought
π	(p)	pet
ρ	(r)	red
σ, ς	(s)	see
(before voiced consonant e.g. κόσμος)	(z)	haze
τ	(t)	top
υ	(i)	meet
φ	(f)	fat
χ	(x)	loch
(before i & e sounds)	(ç)	hew
ψ	(ps)	apse
ω	(ɔ)	bought

Vowel combinations

ει, οι υι	(i)	meet
(like η, ι, υ)		
αι	(e)	ten
(like ε)		
ου	(u)	boot
αυ	(af)	after
(before voiced sounds)	(av)	have
ευ	(ef)	left
(before voiced sounds)	(ev)	ever
ηυ	(if)	leaf
(before voiced sounds)	(iv)	leave

Consonant combinations

γγ	(ng)	finger
γξ	(nks)	lynx
γχ	(nx, nç)	
γκ (initial)	(g)	go
(medial)	(g, ng, nç)	
μπ (initial)	(b)	bed
(medial)	(b, mb, mp)	
ντ (initial)	(d)	dog
(medial)	(d, nd, nt)	
τζ	(dz)	adze

BIBLIOGRAPHY FOR CHAPTER ONE

Works marked with an asterisk are recommended for general reading.

Language
W. Allen *Vox Graeca. A Guide to the Pronunciation of Classical Greek* (3rd Ed. Cambridge 1987)

Γ. Μπαμπινιώτης Συνοπτικὴ Ἱστορία Τῆς Ἑλληνικῆς Γλώσσας (Athens 1985)

*R. Browning *Medieval and Modern Greek* (2nd Ed. Cambridge 1983)

C.D. Buck *The Greek Dialects* (Chicago 1955)
A Dictionary of Selected Synonyms in the Principal Indo-European Languages (Chicago 1965)

*J. Chadwick *The Decipherment of Linear B* (2nd Ed. Cambridge 1967)

P.S. Costas *An Outline of the History of the Greek Language, with particular emphasis on the Κοινή and the subsequent periods* (Chicago 1979)

*J.T. Hooker *Linear B, An Introduction* (Rev. printing Bristol 1983)

R. Katičič *Ancient Languages of the Balkans* (The Hague 1976)

*L.R. Palmer *The Greek Language* (London 1980)

G. Thomson *The Greek Language* (Cambridge 1960)

A.G. Woodhead *The Study of Greek Inscriptions* (2nd Ed. Cambridge 1981)

Reading Greek Joint Association of Classical Teachers' Greek Course (Cambridge 1978)

Historical and Cultural Background
V.R. d'A. Desborough *The Greek Dark Ages* (London 1972)

M.I. Finley *Early Greece: The Bronze and Archaic Ages* (London 1981)

*Fontana History of the Ancient World
O. Murray *Early Greece* (1980)
J.K. Davies *Democracy and Classical Greece* (1978)
F.W. Walbank *The Hellenistic World* (1981)

J.T. Hooker *Mycenaean Greece* (London 1977)

L.H. Jeffery *The Local Scripts of Archaic Greece* (Oxford 1961)

R. Pfeiffer *History of Classical Scholarship* (Oxford 1968)

115

*L.D. Reynolds and N.G. Wilson *Scribes and Scholars* (2nd Ed. Oxford 1978)

*J. de Romilly *A Short History of Greek Literature* (Translated by L. Doherty) (Chicago 1985)

A. Snodgrass *Archaic Greece* (London 1980)
  The Dark Age of Greece (Edinburgh 1971)

E. Vermeule *Greece in the Bronze Age* (Chicago 1964)

BIBLIOGRAPHY FOR CHAPTERS TWO TO FIVE

This bibliography does not include details of the Greek texts but lists all the other works which I have used in preparing the book and additional works which can be recommended to the reader.

The Greek Language
Ν. Ἀνδριώτης Ἐτυμολογικὸ Λεξικὸ τῆς Κοινῆς Ἑλληνικῆς (Salonica 1951, 1967)
B.F.C. Atkinson *The Greek Language* (London 1933)
Γ. Μπαμπινιώτης Συνοπτικὴ Ἱστορία τῆς Ἑλληνικῆς Γλώσσας (Athens 1985)
R. Browning *Medieval and Modern Greek* (Cambridge 1983)
Γ.Ν. Χατζιδάκις Σύντομος Ἱστορία τῆς Ἑλληνικῆς Γλώσσης (Athens 1915)
P. Mackridge *The Modern Greek Language* (Oxford 1985)
J.T. Pring *The Oxford Dictionary of Modern Greek* (Oxford 1982)
G. Thomson *The Greek Language* (Cambridge 1960)
A Manual of Modern Greek (London 1967)
A. Thumb *A Handbook of the Modern Greek Vernacular* (Edinburgh 1912) (First German edition 1895)
Μ. Τριανταφυλλίδης Νεοελληνικὴ Γραμματικὴ (Athens 1941)

Anthologies and Translations
Medieval and Modern Greek Poetry, An anthology by C. A. Trypanis (Oxford 1951)
The Penguin Book of Greek Verse, with plain prose translations of each poem (ancient Greece to modern Greece) edited by C.A. Trypanis (London 1971)
Six Poets of Modern Greece (Cavafy, Sikelianos, Seferis, Antoniou, Elytis, Gatsos) translated and introduced by Edmund Keeley and Philip Sherrard (London 1960)
Four Greek Poets (Cavafy, Seferis, Elytis, Gatsos), poems chosen and translated by Edmund Keeley and Philip Sherrard (London 1966)
Crusaders as Conquerors: The Chronicle of the Morea, translated by H.E. Lurier (Columbia 1964)

Odysseus Elytis, The Axion Esti, translated by Edmund Keeley and George Savidis. (London 1980)

V. Kornaros, The Erotocritos, translated by Theodore Stephanides (Athens 1984)

The Memoirs of General Makriyannis, translated by H.A. Lidderdale (Oxford 1966)

Kostis Palamas, The Twelve Lays of the Gipsy, translated by George Thomson (London 1969)

Literary Criticism

R. Beaton *Folk Poetry of Modern Greece* (Cambridge 1980)

P. Bien *Constantine Cavafy* (1964) (Columbia essays on modern writers)
Nikos Kazantzakis (1972) (Columbia essays on modern writers)
Kazantzakis and the Linguistic Revolution in Greeek Literature (Princetown 1972)

C.T. Dimaras *A History of Modern Greek Literature* (English edition) (London 1974)

R.A. Fletcher *Kostes Palamas, A Great Modern Greek Poet* Athens 1984

L. Politis *A History of Modern Greek Literature* (Oxford 1973)

P. Sherrard *The Marble Threshing Floor* (London 1956. Athens 1980)

Historical and Cultural Background

The Cambridge Medieval History IV. *The Byzantine Empire*

J. Campbell and P. Sherrard *Modern Greece* (London 1968)

N. Cheetham *Mediaeval Greece* (Yale and London 1981)

M. Llewellyn Smith *The Great Island—A Study of Crete* (London 1965)
Ionian Vision–Greece in Asia Minor 1919–1922 (London 1973)

R. Loverance *Byzantium* (British Museum 1988)

A.A. Pallis *Greek Miscellany. A collection of essays on medieval and modern Greece* (Athens 1964)

D. Pentzopoulos *The Balkan Exchange of Minorities and Its Impact upoon Greece* (Paris 1962)

A. Toynbee *Constantine Porphyrogenitus and His World* (Oxford 1973)

A. Toynbee *The Greeks and Their Heritages* (Oxford 1981)

C.M. Woodhouse *The Greek War of Independence* (London 1952. New York 1975)
Modern Greece. A Short History (3rd edition. London 1984)